Chronicles
of
Love
&
Confusion

Author ~ Shari Nocks Gladstone
Illustrator ~ Candace Staulcup

First Edition

Biographical Publishing Company
Prospect, Connecticut

Chronicles of Love & Confusion

First Edition

Published by:

Biographical Publishing Company
35 Clark Hill Road
Prospect, CT 06712-1011

Phone: 203-758-3661   Fax: 603-853-5420   e-mail: biopub@aol.com

Copyright © 1999 by Shari Nocks Gladstone
First Printing 1999
PRINTED IN THE UNITED STATES OF AMERICA

Library of Congress Cataloging-in-Publication Data

Gladstone, Shari Nocks, 1930-
    Chronicles of Love & Confusion / Shari Nocks Gladstone ;
illustrator, Candace Staulcup. – 1st ed.
        p.   cm.
    ISBN 0-9637240-2-9 (pbk. : alk. paper)
1. Gladstone, Shari Nocks, 1930- – Childhood and youth.
2. Jews – New York (State) – New York Biography.
3. Manhattan Beach
(New York, N.Y.) Biography.
4. Manhattan Beach (New York, N.Y.) – Ethnic relations.
    I. Title.   II. Title: Chronicles of Love and Confusion.
F128.9.J5G55 1999
974.7'1004924'0092–dc21
[B]   99-32288
                                                         CIP

Table of Contents

Part 3 — The Teen Years

The author at two years of age

This book is lovingly
dedicated to Yette and her progeny.

PREFACE

May I say a few words about memory-inspired writing that I hope you read before you get into the stories that follow?

These bits and pieces have root in long-ago happenings and are more a reflection of feelings than they are a study in accuracy. I daresay, some of the events you are about to stumble over may have happened in some other way, or in some other form. Perhaps they are just the seeds of long dormant memories that have awakened and come to flower in this author's imagination.

The purpose of this collection of memory-inspired writings is not to tell the story of my life. Far from it. It is more like an attempt at painting a picture of a place and time in history that I was privileged to occupy.

The period between The Great Depression and the end of World War II was my growing-up time. My growing-up place: Manhattan Beach, a corner of the borough of Brooklyn in New York City, encircled by the waters of Sheepshead Bay and the Atlantic Ocean. Within that circle, we lived as if in a cocoon of family life and neighborliness based on common culture and ethnicity. It was a Jewish world. In the beginning — the Depression Years — we were poor, but I never knew it. In the end, we were rich, but for me it was merely our way of life. The sometimes puzzling events of the world all but passed over me. Rich or poor. Peace or war. It didn't seem to matter very much. We were who we were, and that was that! Little else mattered beyond the cycle of our days.

Was it unique? I don't know. Perhaps only in the way that all childhood times and places seem unique when we look at them, in memory, through the wrong end of the telescope.

You will notice that a good part of life seems to have taken place at the dining room table or in the kitchen. Cooking aromas filled the house from morning to nightfall. Women were preoccupied with meal preparation. There were no cookbooks. Recipes handed down from generation to generation were part of our oral history. Food was both an expression of love and of well being. Men were proud of their plump wives and of their own portly bodies.

As it was important to set a good table, it was also important to be well dressed. A lot of time and money was allotted to shopping for and buying clothing, furs and jewelry — again a very public display of affluence. There were rigid rules of behavior. Children were brought up carefully: taught to be circumspect, to turn a proper face to the world, and to bring no discredit to the family.

As keenly as I remember the smell of simmering chicken soup, I remember the cadence of the speech and the way adults switched from English to Yiddish when they didn't want the younger generation to understand what they were saying. But we learned most of the key words anyway. They came flooding back into my conscious mind as, so many years later, I started to write about those times. I only hope that I have remembered and used them correctly.

Finally, this is the story of a Jewish family traveling the road from immigrant status to assimilation into the American mainstream. It wasn't always an easy journey.

Shari Nocks Gladstone
Dix Hills, New York
January 1999

Part 1
Before I was Born

1

CHUTZPAH*

Yette and Nachum — my paternal grandparents — were expecting a child. The women of the shtetl thought it might be twins.

They were right.

When Yette's time came, it was discovered that a pair of twins had been intertwined in the womb. During the birthing, with only a village midwife to assist, one baby

---

*See glossary

died and the other was severely maimed. This was Clara. Her legs and hips were hopelessly misshapen. She was fragile and very, very tiny. She cried all the time. Her mother, Yette, hovered over her, massaging her damaged body and praying for her survival.

There were other children. An older daughter and a healthy little boy. Though rejoicing over their growing family, Yette and Nachum, also discussed life and current events as they understood them. Soon, they feared, it would become time for them to take their place amongst the hordes of people fleeing Europe. It would be time to leave Roumania and go to America. What choices did they have? They could remain in the ghetto and, as Jews, live always in fear. Or they could cross the Atlantic Ocean to the United States — and freedom. As difficult as it all seemed, there was really only one decision to be made.

But an enormous problem existed! What could the family do about Clara? She was now a little girl, a toddler. Adorable — and ever so smart — but undeniably a cripple. By now everyone had heard of the rigorous physical examinations that were a part of the Ellis Island experience. Truly, the doorway to the New World was firmly shut in the face of anyone who was not physically perfect.

Yette was in a quandary! She was again pregnant and had so much on her mind. She could not leave her damaged daughter behind, nor could she delay the rest of the family any longer. Conditions were dangerous. Their time to leave had come. She was heavy with child and had several little ones crowding against her legs. The third oldest, but undoubtedly the smallest, was Clara. What was to be done? Only a daring and imaginative solution could resolve this terrible dilemma!

The newest baby was born on the boat. When the time came for the family to disembark, all of the children were instructed on how to behave. Silence was imperative. The usually gregarious little ones were warned not to say a single word. Clara was wrapped up in swaddling clothes as if still an infant. She, too, was cautioned not to speak. As tiny as she was, and entirely wrapped in the style of the times, she was carried through the morass that was Ellis Island and passed off as yet another baby. Her twisted legs were never unwrapped, nor did they touch the ground. With the new little boy, Daniel, in one arm and the disguised Clara in the other, Yette and her "twins" walked into the United States with Nachum at her side.

Their duplicity was successful. The family remained intact and a life of freedom began for all of them.

2

RIVKA — A LOVE STORY

About a hundred years ago — give or take — and not too many years after his arrival in this country, my paternal grandfather died of a sudden and terrible illness. He had been a tailor. It is my understanding that, financially, he had done rather well for an immigrant. There was always food on the table. The children were adequately dressed. The rent was paid.

According to the only picture of him that I have ever seen, Nachum had brown hair, a round face and a big moustache. He had fathered many children, but only seven of them lived past infancy. At the time of his death, they were still quite small. Yette — his wife and my grandmother — was bereft and alone. Without too much cash. Without too many friends. Without competency in the language and customs of her new land. What was she to do?

Somehow, a funeral was arranged. The family went to the synagogue dressed in good clothing. The children behaved as well as could be expected. The Cantor intoned the ancient chants and the Rabbi said the holy words.

Yette wanted to be sure that Nachum was honored appropriately. All the traditions were observed. The proper food was prepared. The mirrors were covered. The plain wooden benches were set out. The clothes of the mourners were torn in the usual way. The shiva* began.

As is the way, family and friends gathered after the funeral for the first day of this traditional, week-long ceremony of mourning. Yiddish was spoken in the European way — with a few words of English, Roumanian, Russian and French thrown in. It was all so sad.

"Such a young man," the guests murmured.
"So many children."
"What will the widow do?"
"How will she feed them all?"
"Who will pay the rent?"
"What would become of them?"

There was a soft knock at the door that went almost unheard in the midst of all this conversation. A timid young woman waited outside, surrounded by packages and

*See glossary.

bundles. It was a sight familiar to all of those present. Another immigrant. Another new arrival. Another one "right off the boat." Another greenhorn.

It was Rivka.

No more than 15 years old at the time, she had traveled alone from Roumania to the United States, with plans to stay, for a time, with a cousin she had heretofore never met. Nachum. Arriving, as she did, in the midst of the shiva for her only known relative in this strange land, she was understandably devastated. She had no words. Only tears. Tears for the unknown Nachum. Tears for herself. What would happen to her now? Where would she go? Who would take care of her?

Yette rose to the occasion. In her house slippers — the only footwear properly worn at shiva — she moved towards the frail, little newcomer. She hugged her. They held each other. They mingled their tears. Yette was clear: Nachum's cousin was her cousin, and despite the problems of the moment, she welcomed her into the family. Whatever they had, Rivka would have. Whatever they ate, she would eat. Whatever their fate — it would be her fate as well.

Several of the littlest children were squeezed into one bed. Room to sleep and a place to put her possessions was arranged. Aunts, uncles, cousins and other more distant relatives were introduced. Friends from The Old Country asked about the health of her parents and other European connections. The amenities were observed. The evening wore on. Eventually, the shiva guests left. The rest of the children were sent to bed. It was time for tea. And for talk.

Despite her grief and her problems, Yette had already sensed that there was more to this situation than met the eye. She boiled the water, and served the tea — as always, in the sturdy glasses that once held the Sabbath candles, and with a spoon in each glass to carry off the heat. The oversized sugar bowl was placed on the table. In the Roumanian manner, each woman took a sugar cube between her teeth and sipped the hot beverage through the sweetness. Yette's questions were gentle but probing. Rivka's story began to unfold. For those times, it was a terrible tale.

Rivka had come to this Country, pledged to marry a man that she had never met. In the old way, her marriage had been arranged by a professional match-maker. Her future husband, she had been told, was older than she would have liked and apparently not too attractive. He was, however, known to be of a good family and, above all, to be a good provider. Plans for eventually bringing others in her family to the United States had been discussed. Money had changed hands. Her passage had been paid. Her family had given their promise. Rivka had accepted the arrangement. She was, indeed, betrothed. Committed. A deal had been made in the ancient and honorable way. It could not be set aside.

Many plans had been made. Though the letter detailing all of this had never arrived, Rivka fully expected to stay with her unknown cousin Nachum and his family until the wedding ceremony could take place. Then she would be someone's wife. Beyond this she knew nothing and could not even imagine what such a life would be like. A strange man. An older man. An unknown country. A language she could hardly speak or understand. No friends. And her only kinsman — now deceased. When she embarked from Europe, she had been frightened.

Curious. Resigned. Now the things had become so much worse. She was terrified.

On the boat during the long, crowded, tedious days, and after the terrible bouts of sea-sickness had passed, she met a man and fell in love. A young man. A handsome man. A kind and loving man. His name was Kalman. Awash in emotions, they made love. It was the first time for each of them. They promised themselves to each other. Forever. Come what may. Now, what was she to do? For all she knew — and truthfully, she didn't know much — she could be carrying Kalman's child.

Yette, the older and more experienced of the two women, tried to think through Rivka's dilemma with her. They talked and talked, and drank more tea. They went to bed and tried to sleep. Tomorrow they would talk more. Soon they would decide what was to be done. After all, life goes on. It must.

As I was to learn throughout my girlhood and later life, there were two distinct sides to my grandma Yette. On the one hand she was most practical, and on the other, most romantic. Her solution to the problem at hand reflected this. Under her tutelage and guidance, a decision was made and her newly-discovered young cousin went forward into a new life.

A promise was broken. Sobeit! It must have happened before! It surely would happen again!

Within days, Rivka and Kalman left the USA and, with no more than the clothes on their backs, headed together for Cuba. Again, an all but unknown family connection was contacted, befriended them and helped them to get started. (One suspects Yette's hand in this!) They changed their names to reflect the culture of their new country. Rivka became Riva and Kalman became Carlos. They had a daughter. They worked hard and prospered. They lived well.

When revolution disrupted Cuba, they fled. First, they smuggled their daughter and her nursemaid out of the country. It seemed to be the way things were being done at the time. Then, they walked, as nonchalantly as they could, away from their home, leaving all of their accumulated possessions behind. They strolled hand in hand. They made it to the airport. No longer young — and again with no more than the clothes they wore — they made their way back to the USA. And started over for the third time.

They sheltered the nursemaid who had helped rescue their daughter. She lived with them for the rest of her life. Their daughter became an educated American woman. There were grandchildren. As I write this, Riva and Carlos are old and ever so fragile. But, they are still together and they love each other dearly to this very day.

3

WHAT'S IN A NAME . . .

After Nachum died, Yette bore the full responsibility for keeping the family together. It then consisted of herself and the seven children who had survived infancy: Estelle, Julius, Clara, Albert, Daniel — born on the boat — and Dorothy and Henry — born in America. Their Roumanian last name was unspellable, and all but unpronounceable, in the English language. The closest I can come to it here, phonetically spelled, is: Nochminavicce.

Grandma was tall and imposing, and very much alone. To her chagrin, though an educated woman, she could neither speak, read nor write in the language of her new country. She studied, but learning was slow. Like most of her compatriots, she resorted to Yiddish, the middle European lingua franca, and did the best she could. She wanted to blend in, to assimilate, to become part of the mainstream. She wanted to be a citizen. As time went by it was often her older children who pointed out the ways to become "more American." Often, to conceal her language deficits, her solutions to problems were quite inventive.

There came a day when Henry, the youngest of the children, had to be registered for school. It was an important day, but it was not something that Yette felt she could do and still maintain her dignity. She felt that she couldn't fill out the required forms and couldn't communicate with the school authorities in the proper way. It was unseemly. It was too much.

Not one of the five older children, already through grade school, into high school and out in the streets earning money, was available to her on that day. There was only Dorothy. The next-to-the-youngest. The quiet one. She was in second grade, spoke beautiful English and could read and write as well as anyone her age, if not better. Sadly, she could do these specific things far better than her mother.

And so, as instructed, on the first day of school a serious and self-important Dorothy took her little brother's hand and led him to the principal's office.

"This," she said, "is my brother, Henry Nocks. I'm supposed to register him in school."

The principal stared.

"Nocks?" she queried, her voice sharp and impatient. "What is this? What do you mean? What are you saying — and what is this, Nocks? And who is this Nocks?"

Dorothy, all her earlier courage and poise beginning to

crumble, simply repeated: "Henry Nocks. My mother said —" Her lower lip trembled.

The principal asked: "Is this not, then, the brother of Estelle and Julius Nochminavicce?"

"Yes," answered Dorothy, her voice quavering.

"And" — the principal said, loud enough for all to her — "Is this boy not the brother of Clara Nachminovicz, the cripple?"

"Yes." Tears formed.

"Is this, then, also the brother of Albert Nockowitz who attended this school?"

Tears fell.

"And is this child also the brother of Daniel, who graduated with honors? And are you not Dorothy of the same family?"

"Yes. Yes. Yes."

It was all the timid little one could bear. Dorothy ran from the school, leaving young Henry to his fate. Through the streets. To the tenement that was home. To her bedroom. To her bed. She did not return to school for two whole days.

As it is said in the family — Yette emerged from the Lower East Side tenement in her lavender dress and amethyst beads. She went to the school, emanating matriarchal dignity. Somehow, all was resolved.

When all is said and done, what happened to these people?

Henry went to school, following the path that had been carved out by his older siblings, using the Americanized version of the family name. Nocks. He graduated in due course. and became a successful businessman. Dorothy became a second grade teacher.

The other children went their various ways. Daniel — my father — found his niche in the underworld. Al moved to the south and a career as a retail merchant. Clara married and raised several sons before untimely widowhood. Jay was an insurance broker and, sadly, Estelle died at a very early age.

And Yette? When she died she was well past 100 years of age. She could read and write in English. She had become a citizen. She had many grandchildren. She was content. And, finally, twelve living cousins — the grandchildren of Yette and the children of Julius, Clara, Albert, Daniel, Dorothy and Henry, joined together in 1989 to contribute to the "wall of names" in the new Immigrant Hall of Fame on Ellis Island. To honor their grandparents and commemorate their name.

There was one serious problem. They couldn't agree on how to spell it.

BATHTUB GIN

I was only one day old — or thereabouts — when this incident took place. It has the quality of a legend for me since I heard about it again and again as I was growing up.

My father and a man I was later to know as "Uncle Izzy" were celebrating my birth. My mother and I were safely ensconced in the obstetrical wing of Beth Israel hospital in Manhattan and would be there for the traditional two week "lying in" period. The men were at loose ends.

To celebrate, or to amuse themselves — whatever — they decided to make their own whiskey. It was 1930. The Prohibition era. The start of the Great Depression.

Bathtub gin was not uncommon. So they concocted a tubful, somehow, in our small 2-bedroom single bathroom Brooklyn apartment.

To lay aside, for once and for all, the myth that Jews do not drink — let me tell you these Jewish men did. With gusto. Despite prevalent rumors that bathtub gin could cause hair to fall out and teeth to rot, they proceeded to imbibe and enjoy what full they had made. They invited other men. They sang. They laughed. They told dirty stories in Yiddish. They had a ball.

Of course, during their spree, my brother and our housekeeper, had nowhere to bathe and little to no privacy for other bathroom needs. It got a little touchy. Mary — an extremely stern newly-arrived Irish immigrant — was not too pleased. Nor was she pleased to find strange men

"sleeping it off" on the living room couch. Or eating salami and knishes out of paper bags on the gleaming mahogany dining room table.

So, she told Aunt Pauline. Aunt Pauline told her friend Sadie. Sadie told just about everyone she knew in the garment center. The word finally reached Aunt Etta, my mother's older sister. She, in turn, went to the hospital and told my mother. What a scene!

By the time we came home, the tub was cleaned, scoured and polished. Not a trace of their monumental binge remained. Not even the smell.

Part 2
Early Childhood

5

SCHOOL DAYS

School was starting. To the little ones who were entering for the first time, the four-story grey stone building looked cold and intimidating. Forbidding. Even dangerous. The concrete schoolyard that encircled it was surrounded by a high wire fence. Older, bigger children were running and shouting, playing games that as yet had no meaning. It was all very frightening.

One by one the smallest children arrived, accompanied by mothers, nannies or older siblings. Some of them hung back as they approached the front entrance, dragging their heels and being forcibly propelled by their escorts. Faces set, a few walked forward as stiffly and silently as mini-

automatons. Others cried and clung to their companions.
As the little ones entered the building, they were greeted
by the principal, escorted by a monitor to the Kindergarten
classroom and shown to an assigned seat. In most cases,
they managed to part from their familiar people and bravely
enter the designated area on their own. One or two were
so terribly frightened, so very tearful, that it was
considered prudent for their parents to accompany them to
the classroom for a short while.

One such little boy was named Barry. He simply could
not stop crying. Nor sobbing. Bawling. Howling. Nor
would he release the grip he had on his mother's hand. His
fingers dug into her wrist, the pressure turning her skin
white, then red. His new brown woolen jacket was soaked
with tears and nose-drip. Once in the classroom, his
agitation increased.

Perhaps a dozen pupils had already assembled and,
terrified or not, were sitting quietly in their seats. The
classroom was filled with sunlight and interesting objects
that began to catch their interest. More children arrived.
The teacher was motherly and kind, greeting them warmly
and speaking to each of them by name. One by one they
responded and began the metamorphosis from scared baby
to student. All but Barry.

With the other parents finally gone, the teacher, Mrs.
Mendelson, offered Barry's mother a seat. She loomed
large in the child-size wooden chair. Despite her obvious
discomfort, Barry climbed into her lap and clung there. His
wild sobbing had subsided, replaced by intermittent
hiccups, but his face was red and tear-streaked and his
nose still dripped. He sniffled and snuffled. He was not a
pretty sight. The morning wore on. The well-prepared
teacher announced a Science lesson and displayed an

interesting collection of sea shells, beach glass and pretty stones. The children were captivated, passing the glittering bits from hand to hand. Barry still sat on his mother's lap and watched, but his hold was relaxing. One could see the tenseness beginning to leave his body. Mrs. Mendelson, thinking that she could now safely reach out to him, produced an exceptionally shiny, mica-touched stone for him to examine. Shyly, he touched it. Then held it. And, responding slowly to Mrs. Mendelson's experienced class-room technique, he eventually managed to stand and take one small step away from his mother.

"Well," said Mrs. Mendelson. "That's wonderful. I'm so pleased that you're no longer as frightened as you were before."

"But I am," hiccupped Barry. "I'm as scared as scared. But all my tears are used up for now."

As Mrs. Mendelson engaged the little boy in eye-to-eye conversation, she subtly motioned for his mother to leave the room. The other children were silent as they watched the drama unfolding in front of them with fascination.

Well, Barry," said the teacher. "Perhaps, then, you can tell us all why you're so very scared. Maybe we can get together as a class and do something about it. Maybe we can help you."

The sobs were threatening to take over again but Barry managed to gasp: "I'm scared 'cause this is a school and I don't know how to read."

"Oh my dear," comforted Mrs. Mendelson, hugging his shoulders lightly. "You don't have to worry about that. This is only Kindergarten. Nobody here has learned how to read yet."

She turned Barry to face the class, and asked aloud "If anyone in this room knows how to read, please raise your hand!"

The room was quiet. It was an intense moment. You could feel the emotions emanating from the other children. For the first time, they were together — a class reaching out to a fellow student who appeared to be in trouble and in pain. Then, breaking the spell, a hand shot up. A little girl with brown curls and a big bow in her hair was jumping up and down in her seat. Her entire body was alive with movement, bubbling over with eagerness and excitement. She kept waving her hand in the air, reaching up as high as she could.

"I can read," she said. "My brother learned me. I can read anything."

Barry shrieked. Mrs. Mendelson held him, speaking to him softly. She buzzed for a monitor at the same time. Barry's mother had to be called back to the classroom. Even the principal came. It was a mess.

More than 60 years have passed. To this day, I still wish I hadn't raised my hand!

6

ECONOMICS

Third grade was an exciting time. There was so much to do and so much to learn. I loved it. I knew I was one of the smartest kids in "3 A" and, in my own eyes, I was popular as well as smart. An eight-and-a-half year old just a little too big for her britches. Until the day my schoolgirl world came crashing down.

It started simply enough. Mrs. Levine was talking to the class about economics. It was a new topic and most of the children were attentive. She told us about the different ways that men worked in order to support their families. To illustrate the point, she began to ask each one of the students what kind of work his or her father did for a living.

"Let's give Jason a turn," she said, starting with the slowest boy — the one in the last seat of the last row. His father owned the local butcher shop.

"My father makes meat," he said.

Mrs. Levine went down the rows, asking each child the same question. Barbara's father was the doctor and Irene's the dentist. Richard's father was a professor in Brooklyn College and Margie's father was the Rabbi. I was so fascinated by all that was going on, I didn't realize that my turn would be coming soon. As it turned out I was last, since I was sitting in the coveted First Row, First Seat. This honor was mine for the week since I had gotten the highest mark in the last spelling test.

My turn came.
"Well, Miss Nocks, what does your father do?"
I looked at Mrs. Levine, opened my mouth — and nothing came out. Embarrassed, I stammered that I didn't know. I hung my head.
"Well, we will ask you again in the morning. "Hopefully you will then be able to tell us how your father earns his money."
When we were filing out of the classroom, Mrs. Levine reminded me. "We'll all be waiting for your answer," she said.
Somehow, I was frightened.
"What does Daddy's do for a living?"
My brother, busy building a crystal radio set, was interrupted by my question.
"Oh-oh!" he replied, "don't ask me, ask Ma." He had a funny look on his face.
"What does my father do for a living?" I asked Mary, the housekeeper.

"Ask your mother," she responded, curtly.

I asked Grandma Yette. She shook her head, refusing to speak.

Then it was dinner time and we were all together. As soon as the brief Hebrew prayers were murmured and the meal served, I asked my father: "Daddy — what do you do for a living?" My question was greeted with silence. My mother got up and headed for the kitchen, muttering "oy gevalt!"* Then my father asked me why I wanted to know. I explained that I was the only one in the class unable to answer the teacher's question, and that I had been terribly embarrassed. My voice was choked and my eyes began filling with tears. "Well," my father was thoughtful; "you can tell them I'm in the shirt business." The next morning, before the salute to the flag and the roll call, that's what I told everyone. Even though I knew it was a lie.

It was several years before I understood that my father was a racketeer. A gambler. And, according to the moral code of the times, a criminal.

As time passed, there were more and more puzzling things to deal with. Once, in school, we learned about Mayor Fiorello H. LaGuardia, "The Little Flower." In our Civics class he was described as a hero, crusading to rid the City of gamblers and racketeers. We saw a picture of him in the newspaper, breaking a slot machine with a baseball bat. But my parents made it clear that they detested him. They would pretend to spit on the floor when they heard his name. I was terribly confused, but said nothing.

Then, my father bought a barber shop — the biggest

---

*See glossary.

one in New York. He made a point of telling me about it, saying that now I could tell everyone what he did for a living. But I knew he wasn't a barber, and wondered. My brother said, "Dim-wit, it's just a front."

When I was approaching my teen years, the basement of our house was re-decorated. The walls were paneled with wood stained light green; my mother called it "pickled pine." A bar was built at one end with a red Formica top. At the other end, an alcove was created with a steel safe concealed in one wall. A desk was placed there. It was built out of the same materials and matched the rest of the room. My brother and I were told never to go near it, never to touch anything on it, never to answer any one of the three phones that it held.

Soon a bald man began to come to the house every day to use this desk and to answer these phones. A nice guy. We called him Uncle Phil.

"You can play in here," he said, "but don't never touch the slips."

These were pieces of white paper that he would tear off a pad and write on, in a cryptic shorthand whenever the phones would ring.

I was often a silent rider in the backseat of the car while we drove to visit relatives in other parts of Brooklyn and on Long Island. My mother and father talked, forgetting that I was there. I absorbed what they said: the horses, Belmont race track, bad odds and what happened in Jersey. Card games. People who went to jail. There was urgency and tension in the things they said to each other. My mother cried. My father sounded angry.

"What else can I do?," he asked her. "Since the Depression, I gotta make a buck, somehow." And, bitterly, "I can see you don't mind spending my dirty money!"

Eventually I overheard that "things were too hot." Soon Uncle Phil stopped coming. The desk was moved into my brother's room since he was going to college. My father became a financial factor, or money lender. "A legitimate occupation," he stressed, as we gathered at the dinner table. My mother raised her eyebrows. I had concluded, over the years, that it was best not to delve too deeply into these things. I kept my conflicts and confusions to myself.

Soon after I left the household, my mother and father became estranged. They rearranged the house and took separate bedrooms. My father moved into the room that had been mine, locating the "pickled" green desk with the red top in the corner by the window. It looked terrible amidst the pink and blue plaid that I had fancied. Not too many years later — still a very young man — he died in that room.

My mother sold the Brooklyn house and relocated to Florida. The green desk went with my brother who had bought a home in rural Pennsylvania and needed furniture. He used it for almost forty years.

Now, the desk has become mine. I painted it white and bought lamps to match the rusty-red Formica top. I put the phone over the shabbiest spot. I cleaned my brother's debris out of the drawers. As I sorted through his things, I kept thinking that I might find one of Uncle Phil's betting slips amid the papers.

These days, when I use the desk, I am very careful. I open the drawers slowly, because they are inclined to stick. But also, because each time I open one, I feel as if I am in danger of releasing the confusing memories of that earlier time.

7

THE FORVITZ*

I was an early reader, mastering written English before I was in Third Grade. I read anything I could find. In the dusty-smelling local library I would stray out of the children's section looking for books I had not yet read, invariably getting caught by a stern and disapproving librarian. She called my mother, who told my father. I think he was supposed to be upset but instead was delighted. He tested my skills in his own way. I sat on his lap at the head of the dining room table as we read the *Daily News* together. Headlines. News. Sports. Comics.

---

*See glossary.

When I stumbled over a difficult word, he would supply the correct pronunciation and his version of the meaning. Even though I could read the words, the concepts were confusing and often far beyond my understanding.

Grandma used to visit from time to time. It was her way to go from one of her children's homes to another, stay for awhile, then move on. From Manhattan to Brooklyn to the Bronx. She made her rounds. When she stayed at our house, she slept in my room. I loved her but didn't like that at all. She smelled like an old lady and made strange noises in her sleep. The first time I saw her getting undressed, I was terribly frightened. When she removed her hair net, it looked to me as if the top of her head had come off. I waited until she went to the bathroom to investigate. I could see, then, that to combat her thinning hair she had saved the strands that had fallen out and molded them into a puff that remained inside the net and amplified her coiffure.

Of course, she was the one who discovered that I woke up at all hours of the night and read, using a flashlight under the bedcovers for illumination. She disapproved, thinking it was bad for my eyes. I attempted to convince her not to tell my parents. She agreed, but drove a hard bargain. She would not tell, if I would teach her to read.

This is how we did it.

When I returned home from school, she would put a few pennies in my hand and send me to the local candy and stationery store to pick up her copy of the Yiddish newspaper, *The Jewish Daily Forward* (which she pronounced as "The Forvitz.") She always gave me one or two cents too much so I could buy candy. It took me twice as long to browse the penny candy counter then it did to pick up her newspaper.

Then I would read from the previous night's copy of the *Daily News*, or *The Mirror*, while she would find the same news story in her paper. We sat on the edge of the bed, side by side. I would read slowly, stopping at certain key words. She would find them in her paper, then look over my shoulder to see what they looked like in English. We did very well with the headlines. In the actual stories, there was a lot of confusion and disagreements. Grandma was inclined to believe the Yiddish rather than the English versions.

I wondered why Grandma was struggling so desperately to learn English. After a while she confided in me. It was a requirement for becoming a citizen of the United States of America. I was impressed with the importance of our task. So, we read in tandem, through many long afternoons. Then, one night at the dinner table, she took my father's copy of *The News* right out of his hand. Before he could object, she haltingly read it out loud from cover to cover.

We applauded. We laughed. We hugged and kissed her. My mother brought her a brimming glass of her favorite kosher* wine with the pastries. My father tousled her hair, then bent over her hand and kissed it as if she was a princess. In time he took her to take the dreaded citizenship test. She passed.

---

*See glossary.

8

TONGUE

When we were kids, a meal served often in our house was tongue. Smoked beef tongue. It was served either hot or cold, with an assortment of garnishes. I loved it. Especially cold.

I remember going to visit a farm for the first time in my life. I was about 5 or 6 years old. The farm belong to my mother's uncle. I never knew his name. In the European way, we just called him "Uncle." Everybody did.

It was at this farm that I saw my first cow. I had

already been told that beef was the meat from a cow and it was good to eat — as opposed to pork, the meat from a pig, that was not alright to eat. Never. I kept looking at the cow. She was chewing her cud, as cows do. I waited and waited for her to stick her tongue out. I wanted to see it. Frankly, I couldn't see how such a large piece of meat was contained inside her mouth. She looked at me placidly, chewing and switching the flies away with her tail. I watched for hours but was never able to see her tongue.

I was getting obsessed with the subject. One night, just before dinner was served, I got caught standing on the toilet in the downstairs bathroom with my shoes on. I was trying to be tall enough to see in the mirror over the sink. When my mother found me I was sticking my tongue out and sort of twirling it around while looking in the mirror. I got yelled at.

But I still couldn't figure it out.

9

THE BIRTHDAY PARTY

When I was a kid — 9 or 10 years old — birthday parties were a big thing. Doting Jewish parents indulged their children with catered food, thematic decorations and ice cream frozen in shapes to complement the decor. It was as if they vied with one another in providing unique amusements for their children's special days.

One party became grander than the next. A pony and cart was fairly commonplace. So were rides in antique cars or in a rented, portable merry-go-round. An organ grinder with a monkey dressed in a red jacket and hat had been to several parties. Broadway shows and dinners in

restaurants in New York City or a hockey games at Madison Square Garden had all been done. Actually, a few of the older kids had even celebrated their birthdays in Israel with one or two of their friends along for fun.

Though my parents were about the flashiest couple in the neighborhood, I had never had that kind of party. I wanted one so much there was an ache inside me. So, one day, I blurted it all out to my cousin. She told her mother who, in turn, told mine.

Shortly thereafter, I came home from school one afternoon and discovered my father interviewing a magician in our living room. The man was displaying his costume: a black cape lined with red silk, a black cane and a black top hat. And an absolutely adorable bunny rabbit, with pink-lined ears and a pink nose, who popped out of the hat when it was rapped with the cane. He let me try it. I was enchanted. Then my mother told me that the vanilla ice cream was to be specially frozen, shaped like bunny rabbits with pink ears and noses.

I was deliciously happy. The ache inside me was gone. I proceeded to tell every friend I had in the neighborhood. They were all invited.

That year my birthday, March 8th, dawned with cold, gray skies and rapidly falling snow. Despite my tears, the party was canceled. My mother made many phone calls. It was too icy. It was too dangerous. People might get in accidents. Children could get sick. The magician might not be able to make the trip.

I wandered around the house dressed in my rose-pink party dress. It had a white bow at the neck, the ends of which hung almost down to the hem. Much to my mother's dismay, I also put on my brand new black patent leather T-strap Mary Janes. And sat, gulping back my sobs, in a corner behind the door of the housekeeper's bedroom. That was where I usually hid out when I absolutely did not want to be found. In a little while, I dozed off, my head on the window sill.

When I awoke the snow had stopped and the sun was shining brightly. Despite my mother's frantic calls, the ice cream had nonetheless been delivered. The 24 little bunnies were melting in the sink, turning into unattractive gooey pink and white lumps.

I went outside and walked, heartbroken, through every puddle I could find. I shuffled my feet in the muddy water. I ruined my brand new Mary Janes. Nobody even hollered at me.

There were other birthdays and other parties, but nothing was ever the same.

10

BAR MITZVAH*

We had some great places to play after school. One was the schoolyard itself, about 6 blocks away. It had a giant tree in it with many separate trunks, and was the perfect place for Ringaleevio and Hide-And-Seek. We were also allowed to play in the big lot outside the tiny, old Catholic church on the corner. The priest was tiny and old, too. His congregation numbered no more than a half-dozen parishioners. I think he enjoyed having us there to alleviate his loneliness. He taught us to roast "mickeys" — potatoes baked in a hole in the ground filled with charcoal. Father

*See glossary.

Wallace supervised so we didn't burn ourselves but we had to bring our own salt. We carried it in our pockets folded inside pieces of waxed paper. On cold, rainy days he let us into the church where we would tell ghost stories sitting in the back pew. I am reasonably sure that our parents never knew about that.

Undoubtedly the best place to play was in the street right outside our house. It ran from Oriental Boulevard to the Atlantic Ocean and was a designated play street. Around 9 o'clock every morning, when most of the men had left for work, a patrol car with 2 policeman in it would pull up. The cops would roll a stanchion into the middle of the street. It told the world that no cars were allowed to enter without the permission of a homeowner and — should that happen — they were not permitted to drive any faster than 20 miles an hour. They would return in the evening and roll the stanchion back to its place at the curb.

Some enterprising kid had once painted a permanent grid for "potsy" — or hopscotch — at one end of the street. In the main, that was where the girls congregated. Further down the street were two cages, or goals, for the all but continuous street hockey game. It was played on roller skates. When the guys didn't have enough players to field 2 equal teams, they often drafted one of the girls to fill in as goalie. Anyway, my brother, Arnie, was an avid hockey player.

When he passed his twelfth birthday, however, things changed. He was to make his Bar Mitzvah[*] synonymous with his thirteenth birthday. That meant that 3 afternoons each week, he had to pass up his hockey game and

---

*See glossary

present himself at the Rabbi's* study to delve into Jewish law, learn to read and speak in Hebrew, memorize certain passages from the Torah* and prepare his Bar Mitzvah speech. He hated it — but there was no recourse. As he studied, my mother planned the festivities that would take place to celebrate his symbolic entrance into manhood.

Right after the service there would be the traditional get together in the basement of Temple Bethel — an open house where wine and honey cake were served to anyone and everyone in the congregation. My mother would have liked to plan an elaborate repast, in a hotel in the city, to which only close friends and family would be invited. My brother was so vehemently opposed that he cried and staged a real tantrum. Not even the promise of many, many presents could change his mind. Plans had to be scaled down to a formal dinner party in our own home.

During the actual Bar Mitzvah service, I was surprised to see how small and delicate Arnie was, standing at the bema* amongst the older men. In the street, aiming hockey pucks at me when I filled in as goalie, he appeared formidable.

He learned Hebrew slowly. It was nothing like the Yiddish that most of the adults spoke from time to time. We were familiar with that and had learned, hit or miss, enough words to understand what was being said, especially those things our parents didn't want us to hear. But now — with Hebrew — there was a way to say things the older folks might not understand.

The first phrase Arnie doped out for himself, using his

---

*See glossary.

Hebrew to English dictionary, was to become a part of our secret sibling vocabulary. It was a warning of sorts: "Quiet! here comes the Mother!" We used it often.

On the day of the Bar Mitzvah, Arnie was so nervous that he threw up on his new white shirt. Luckily, my mother had bought two of them.

LIPSTICK

Back in 1944, lipstick was a big deal. It was the symbolic entrance into the world of women. A world that contained the mysteries of sex, marriage and motherhood. Lipstick was the first step. It came before perfume, high heels, girdles, silk stockings and black sweaters. It came before dating and boys. It came before necking, petting and going all the way.

But, all those things were still denied to me — and so was lipstick.

"You're too young," said my mother.

I raised the question with my aunt, who liked makeup and fancy clothes. "Forget it," she said.

I appealed to my father. I could usually talk him into anything. "Out of the question," he said. "You're still too young. A nice Jewish girl doesn't go around painted."

I compared notes with the girls in my crowd, all 14 years of age. In each and every case parents had said "no lipstick." One or two had been told, not until they were 18. Others might be allowed to use it at 16. In any case, it was impossible to wait that long.

One by one, frightened and trembling, we went into the neighborhood "Five and Dime," wandered about casually, put tentative hands over the glass partition and made a show of looking at the brands and examining the color choices. Then, each of us palmed a tube of Tangee Natural. And stole it.

It was almost our rite of passage.

Then, came the next step. Now that all six of us had our lipstick, how and when could we wear it and not get caught? Not get in trouble? Each of us left the house in the morning, heading for school, with freshly washed faces. Between our various homes and the bus stop, we crouched in convenient bushes, held our coats over our heads for concealment, pulled out little pocket mirrors and carefully applied our lipstick. Once on the bus there were endless discussions regarding its use. Did one simply "follow the lip line" or dare to enhance the fullness of either upper or lower lip by extending the glossy pink stuff beyond the edges? Would that be considered sexy? Or would it just look "fast?"

Trouble was inevitable.

"I'll tell!" said my brother. I gave him my new Tommy Dorsey record to buy his silence.

"I'll tell!" said Judy's little sister. We beat her up.

"What's this pink stuff on your handkerchief?" asked Bubbles' mother, when she was doing the wash.

Eventually, we all got in trouble. Serious trouble. For lying. For stealing. And for wearing lipstick to school. In fact, for wearing it at all.

In time the "powers that be" relented. By age 15 we were all wearing our Tangee Natural. Legitimately. On special occasions. But still no perfume or stockings. And certainly no "going all the way." That was for another time.

12

HOW IRENE GOT HER BRA

There were, loosely, a half-dozen girls in "the crowd," each one of them between eleven and twelve years of age. They were popular girls and good students, bright and alert, who attended the same local public school and spent almost all of their leisure time together.

Their parents were all known to one other, living as they did within the same circumscribed neighborhood, populated by upper middle class Jewish families. They shopped in the same stores, attended the same synagogue, participated in the same community activities and socialized together. The girls behaved in ways similar to their parents. They were close and knew almost everything about each other and about each other's families. They considered themselves a part of the neighborhood elite, privileged children of the "best families" and, though not above a few pranks, were growing up to be expectably prim and proper young ladies.

The acknowledged beauty among the girls was Irene. Her long black hair was straight and shiny, fashionably cut in "bangs" that ended just above her eyebrows. Her features were regular and her nose upturned. (In a Jewish crowd, that was a big deal!) But she was, at the moment, desperately unhappy. She was seated with the other girls, crowded into one booth in the local luncheonette. The others were sharing sodas and giggling. Her face was the only one without a smile. One got the impression that she might well be the butt of the jokes or the subject of the whispered conversations that were taking place around her.

"How come your parents are so old fashioned?" asked Judy. "Mine are bad, but yours just take the cake!"

"I know," answered Irene. "But, tell me, please, what am I supposed to do? I just can't go on like this. It's simply humiliating."

A few of the girls nodded their sympathetic agreement. One or two were still giggling and poking each other, but they gradually began to calm down and soon all presented a most serious demeanor.

"We have to do something about this, but I don't know exactly what" responded Bubbles. "After all, we've sworn a blood oath to stick together forever, so your problem is our problem."

Finally all levity was abandoned. Hard conversations

and problem solving began.

Irene was intensely aware of her burgeoning bosom. Of the six girls in the group, she suddenly had developed the most observable amount of breast tissue. It wasn't much but, compared to her friends — some of whom were not yet menstruating and were "flatter than pancakes" — she felt herself to be "simply enormous." And, here was the bad part, her mother had flatly refused to buy her a bra. Irene, who had up to now received just about everything she had ever wanted, had been denied this one item. Even an emotional appeal to her usually indulgent father had not worked. No bra. Not necessary. Not yet.

The others at the table — Judy, Bubbles, Joan, Robyn and Natalie — presented one idea after another. Some evoked more giggles; others were gravely considered. Finally, a solution of sorts emerged and a plan was agreed upon. If Irene's mother would not buy a bra, then they, the avowed friends, would do so. They would put their monies together and make the purchase as a group.

What a commitment! Though these were the daughters of affluent families, in the style of the times — circa 1942 — their "allowances" were minimal and extra spending money was rare. And money unknown to their benign but very stern parents was practically non-existent. Buying a bra would mean weeks of deprivation for each of them. Weeks of scrimping and saving from their meager supplies of pocket money. Irene recognized the intensity of their friendship. Her eyes were teary as she thanked them profusely. Judy would have to give up her adored Milky Ways, Robyn her comic books and Natalie her nail polish. Fortunately Bubbles and Joan had older sisters from whom they could borrow funds in secret. During the long wait while the money was being amassed, Irene received sage advice from the others: wear loose sweaters and keep your coat on when boys are around. It was the only thing to do.

Within three weeks a sufficient amount was collected: $3.75. The girls had done their groundwork efficiently. Based on exploratory pricing expeditions, they knew that this was the amount of money they would need. Four of the six sworn friends trooped off together. (Robyn was in bed with an earache, and it was thought imprudent to

include Irene in the actual purchasing.) They walked, after school, to the "Five and Dime" in Brighton Beach, the next town. After studying the stock in the lingerie department, and after several conferences and a few vehement arguments right there in the aisles, a decision was made. Bright pink. All lace. Size 32. B cup. Purchased and paid for. The first part of the job was done.

Then Judy snuck the paper wrapped-parcel into her house and, with the help of Bubbles and another girl who lived on her street, wrapped it for mailing. A previously prepared anonymous note was included: "It's about time. (signed) The Boys." The names and address of Irene's parents were lettered on the wrapping paper in an altered handwriting, deliberately smudged and meant to look masculine. Stamps were purchased with the last few pennies and the package was consigned to the mailbox. Now there was nothing to do but wait.

Within a few days Irene had her bras. A day or so after receiving the package, her mother took her into the City to a fine department store. In the teenage girls' department she was made to stand, naked to the waist, in a fitting room while an unsmiling black-clad saleswoman studied her breasts. (Irene was horribly embarrassed. She had never counted on such a thing happening to her.) A choice was made. Six bras were purchased. Plain white cotton. Washable. Size 30. Double A cup.

And soon after that, Irene's enraged parents, resisting her pleading and her tears, registered her in a private all-girls school. She was never again to be a real part of the crowd.

13

HAIRY LEGS

Leslie lived across the street, and the street wasn't all that big. My brother and I could (and did!) actually lie in our beds in our two separate front bedrooms and shout, and she would hear us and respond. Our parents thought this was an awful thing to do. "Common," my mother said. We would be reprimanded.

But what fun it was, on a Sunday morning, to bellow: "Hey, Les. What's your mother got for breakfast?"

"Bagels and Velveeta cheese. And fresh cucumbers from the garden. She says come over."

Cucumbers and Velveeta. An absolutely delicious

combination and a treat we never had at our house.

"We'll be right over. Everyone over here is still sleeping."

Leslie was a year younger than I, kinda weird and lots of fun. She was a stocky girl with curly dark hair and dancing eyes, and what I now recognize as a bad case of low self esteem. She always thought she was ugly. It made her act shy and uncertain, and to occasionally do strange things. At other times she was definite and forceful, like her mother — the star soprano in the highly acclaimed choir at Temple Bethel.

When we were about 11 and 12 years old, Leslie decided it was time to shave her legs. Her mother said "No. You're much too young." (My mother had told me the exact same thing.)

"But I'm so hairy," she said. "It's embarrassing."

"So be embarrassed. You're still too young. Once you start shaving, you'll have to do it all the time. Every week. Once you shave, the hairs get darker and thicker. Like I said, just leave it alone."

"But Maaaa — "

"Enough. The answer is no. That's it. Now get out of my kitchen."

Do you think that was enough for Leslie? No way. Taking my brother and myself into her confidence, she began to scheme, devising a foolproof way to get what she wanted.

The first step was easy. One day after school, she went to the local "Five and Dime" and stole a tube of Nair, a product she had read about that would remove hair painlessly. She smuggled it into the house while her mother was vocalizing at the piano. That part was a snap.

A few days later, expecting the house to be relatively quiet, she asked me to come home with her to try it out. I agreed. As we entered the front door of the Lamberg household, we were greeted by a host of good smells: coffee, cookies, lemon oil, flowers.

"Smells like company" I said.
"Nah. My mom's just cleaning."

Leslie, anxious to get right to her plan, managed somehow, to overlook the two small tables in front of the fireplace, set with the antique tea service, silver spoons and crystal bowls of tea roses.

We scampered into the upstairs bathroom where we remained for over an hour. Not taking too much time to read the directions on the tube, we both slathered our legs with Nair, a depilatory. As promised, the hair wiped off painlessly. Since that worked so well, Les went on to remove the hairs that protruded beyond the lower edge of her bathing suit. Then the hair from her underarms. When she was done, she was almost as hairless as a new born Chihuahua puppy. The only things she spared were her two rather thick eyebrows.

"Hey Les," I said. "It really stinks in here."
"Yeah — kinda like rotten eggs. Or worse."
"I never knew that would happen."
"Neither did I."
"Let's get outta here. It's making me sick to my stomach."

We opened the bathroom door. That's when all hell broke loose.

In the rose-scented parlor, Mrs. Lamberg was

entertaining the members of the temple choir. And the Rabbi.* And the Rebbitsin.* We could hear their voices, and the tinkling sound of silver on china. Then — the Rebbitsin's piercing voice:

"What a strange smell! Is something burning?"
"What is that Millie?"
"I don't know! Let me check the kitchen."
"Oy, oy, oy!" — the Rebbitsin again — "I feel like I'm choking. I have to get out of here."

The group dispersed rapidly, not even finishing their tea. Most of them were holding their hands, or their monogrammed linen handkerchiefs, to their noses.

First Mrs. Lamberg went on the warpath, then dissolved into tears. She sobbed to her husband, who had been summoned home from his office. These children were awful, she told him. Had ruined her tea party. Her standing in the neighborhood. She was humiliated. In time, she told my mother, who told my father.

Let me tell you, there was hell to pay!

---

*See glossary.

14

THE DAY THE PRESIDENT DIED

I can clearly remember an April day more than 50 years ago when, for me, the world stopped turning.

I was roller skating through the quiet Brooklyn streets. The afternoon was waning and my thoughts were shifting from the exciting world of school, boys and contemporary friends, turning towards the more mundane comforts of home. Chicken soup. Dinner with Grandma. Monopoly.

A car pulled up beside me and a casual school friend, a girl in my Civics class, leaned out of her family's sedan. "Did you hear what happened? The President died.

President Roosevelt is dead."

Words were tumbling out of her mouth so quickly that I could hardly assimilate them. I could also hear her father, as if in counterpoint, telling her to hurry up. She managed to repeat her frightening message:

He's dead!" and added "What's gonna happen? What's gonna happen to us?"

The car sped away. I was alone in the twilight street, the frightful bulletin echoing around and through me. I stopped skating. It now seemed somehow sacrilegious. I sat on the curbstone unfastening my skates. The sky was darkening and so was my world. I felt a growing unrest. A dizziness. I had only recently learned about "the Ship of State" and, now, there was no one steering it. Who, indeed, was at the helm? Was there anyone really in charge? The President was dead. I shriveled with fear.

A child of the Depression, I knew no president other than the wheel-chair bound Franklin D. Roosevelt. I knew him from the newsreels: "The Eyes and Ears of the World." I knew him from daily papers and radio. I admired his style, the jaunty way he clenched his cigarette holder between his teeth. I knew about his personal courage in the face of crippling illness. I listened to his "Fireside Chats" and admired the elegant way he shaped his words. He was part of my life. A personage. A man far more distant and more important than the Rabbi at the Shul* or the principal of the high school. For me, there was something almost God-like about him.

I reached home within minutes — tears nibbling at my eyes, hands shaking, heart thumping. My father and a

---

*See glossary.

friend, wearing their overcoats against the chill of the coming night, were on the porch, cigars glowing. In the dusk, a low-tuned radio providing background for their conversation. They were talking about the newspaper columnist, Walter Winchell. I started to speak but the words caught in my throat. In that breath of time I noticed they were smiling. Even laughing. Their behavior was as usual.

I went indoors. My mother was on the telephone making arrangements for a Canasta game. She wiggled her fingers at me and blew me a kiss without stopping her conversation. Grandma was in the kitchen. The bits and pieces of dinner assembled around her were moving in an orderly way towards the dinner table. She kissed my forehead.

"Are you alright, tzostkelleh?* You look so pale."

I said I was fine, only scared because the President had died. In her usual mixture of Yiddish and English she tried to convince me that, though a wonderful man had died, the country would go on. And our lives would go on. I listened to the words she said, but I remained frightened and unsure, still caught in the vortex of my own feelings.

During the evening meal, the adults' conversation included the events of the day. It touched on "poor Eleanor and the children." Then my father's friend offered a prayer for the health of the new president, Harry S. Truman. The men raised their glasses and drank to his well-being. I listened, surrounded by the warmth of our everyday life. By the time we finished the chicken soup with noodles, the roast, the canned peaches, the cookies — magically — the world was again turning.

---

*See glossary.

15

YETTE

Grandma Yette was taller than the other women in the family. Taller than her daughters and taller than some of her sons. Certainly taller than my tiny mother. Taller than me. She was an imposing figure. Her hair had turned gray when she was quite young. As she aged and it got whiter, and her skin seemed to get browner. And browner. Perhaps it was only sunburn!

"Never speak of this," said my mother. "It is not for other people to know." The look on her face was forbidding. Frightening. It followed my father's disclosure: that his mother was a Gypsy. In the face of my mother's comments, there was nothing else to be said. But, I asked myself, if she was a Gypsy, then what am I?

During the early years, whenever my parents left the house, Grandma would ask "Is she gone?" indicating with a movement of her head that she meant my mother. Then she would reach into her carpetbag and bring out a deck of cards wrapped in a handkerchief. "Teshle" she would say. (Once I asked my mother what "teshle" meant. She didn't know. It wasn't, as I had thought, a Yiddish word. It was a Yette word. She must have meant "shuffle.") With her long fingers, she could make the cardboard dance. She manipulated the deck so fast, the cards were a blur. She played incessant games of solitaire; did tricks; taught them to my brother and I.

Wasn't that something for which Gypsies were famous? And she cooked food in ways that nobody else ever did — sometimes even ignoring the shiny new gas stove and resorting to making a mini-fire in our suburban backyard. (This drove my mother to distraction!)

But Yette's hands also powered the silver crochet hook that produced table cloths and bedspreads of the finest lace — one for each of the grandchildren. Creamy lace in intricate patterns. Elegant. Not my idea of Gypsy work. Not something one would expect to see in a Romney caravan.

The concept haunted me. It was somehow glamorous. Exciting. Mysterious. I involved my father in a conversation about it when my mother was not around. "Well, she's only half Gypsy" he said.

That made my a quarter Romney. I began to find that the idea of having Gypsy blood helped me to form an identity for myself. It explained me to me. Some of the things I yearned for. Some of the things that I did. The wildness. The out-of-the-ordinary streak that my mother worked so hard to squash.

So I read everything I could get on Gypsiology, becoming somewhat of an expert. I found things in the books that made the idea more and more possible. More and more exciting. For me, it became a reality. My grandmother was a Gypsy. So I told the world.

Yette walked tall and straight. She carried her head high. She dressed in shades of lavender and wore long Amethyst beads. And she never stayed in one place for long — never really had a home or an apartment of her own. She moved from one of her children's households to another according to some schedule or plan of her own — carrying her homemade carpet bag stuffed with goodies. A huge smoked whitefish. Oranges. Coffee-flavored Dutch candies, called Hopjes, that we hated. Her silver crochet hook. Whatever.

When I was over fifty, in a re-union with my cousins, they de-bunked my theory. Laughed and laughed. Said Grandma's maiden name was Silverman and "this Gypsy business" was just not so. Said my father had been teasing; had made it up. I was devastated, feeling as if I had lost an important piece of my self. This argument went on over several years. As a joke, one of my cousins gave me a tambourine for my sixtieth birthday.

But they hadn't seen the look on my mother's face. Had she been hiding something? I think so. I think she knew the truth.

16

THE ESPLANADE

During the late 1930's and early 40s, every Tuesday night was special. All summer long. From Memorial Day to Labor Day. Year in and year out. Except when it rained.

My growing-up place was our beachfront community, in the southern corner of Brooklyn, encircled by the Atlantic Ocean and Sheepshead Bay. Separating us from the ocean was a concrete walkway called The Esplanade. It stretched the entire length of the neighborhood. Between it and the waves there were huge rocks the size of small tables, dotted with glittering bits of mica. I believe they had been placed there, originally, as part of a public works project in the time of Jacob Riis.

This lovely place often became the repository of tourists' trash — typically, discarded paper bags filled with half- sandwiches and peach pits. Needless to say, the spaces between the rocks became home to huge water rats that sometimes got adventurous and walked right down the street. We lived only three houses from the ocean. When the rats got that far — walking in couples — everybody got upset.

Despite many calls to the political powers-that-be the rodent problem was never resolved. It persisted throughout my childhood. I was cautioned repeatedly to stay clear of the area, but disobeyed more often than not. The flat-topped rocks were just the right size for sunbathing. All the local kids were fearless, clambering — usually barefoot — over the rocks like monkeys. On occasion we dared each other to climb to the bottom of the bulwark and dip our toes into the ocean. (It was a kind of rite of passage. Later, we displayed our feet to each other, sparkling with dried salt.) When we hollered and threw stones at the rats, they would disappear. No problem — until we got caught by a strolling aunt or uncle.

On Tuesday night though, all the rules were relaxed. It was time for fireworks.

In those more gentle times the City, or perhaps the State, funded a public show of fireworks launched from a barge about a mile directly off shore. Except in driving rain, the show started at nightfall. As we approached the time, neighbors — grown ups as well as kids — walked to the end of the street. The adults carried beach chairs, blankets, flash lights, thermos bottles and snacks in brown paper bags. Husbands and wives strolled arm in arm. They chatted with their neighbors. The weather. The sunset. Politics. Kids laughed, told jokes, capered around and tried to reach their chosen spot on the Esplanade before anyone else.

Each and every time, the fireworks began with an extremely loud cannonade, accompanied by random flashes. By then daylight was fading. We had all settled into our favored places, ready to hoot and applaud the bombast.

For the next hour or so, a gorgeous show of lights whizzed through the sky. Cascades of multi-colored brilliance. We had names for each of the displays. (Who had named them — and how long ago — we never knew.) The gathered watchers, almost in unison, would call out the names of each separate one as it lit the sky. Bananas. Wedding rings. Blue fire. Waterfalls. Pinkies. At the end of the show, the loud cannonade was repeated and a hovering fireboat blew its whistle three times. The end. It was our signal to disperse.

Families grouped together and headed for home. Sometimes a few neighbors stopped for conversation and lemonade on our front porch. My eyes were drooping with sleepiness but I tried to stay awake, listening to every word they said in the usual amalgam of Yiddish and English. I can remember the feeling of warmth, dozing, my head nestled against my father's arm. "Gae shluffen, tzotskelleh!" His hand patted my shoulder.

The power and menacing strength of the relentless Atlantic waves eventually broke the Esplanade into pieces — eroding it beyond repair. Finally, World War Two put an end to our Tuesday night ritual. Air raid wardens and black out curtains took its' place.

Part 3
The Teen Years

17

SPIT

One day, at the dinner table, my father made a proclamation of sorts. "A Jewish woman who can type and cook will get along fine in this world!"

When I woke up the next morning there was a streamlined Italian-made portable typewriter in my bedroom, and a "how to do it" book. My father, once the speed typing champion of the City College of New York, had the keys covered with "blinds" so that I couldn't see the letters. I had no choice but to prop the diagram of the keyboard up in front of me and learn to "touch type."

As far as cooking goes, I'd been doing that since I

was little more than seven years old. At that age I spent countless afternoons sitting on the back steps cleaning string beans, shelling peas and grating potatoes for latkes.[*] The older I got, the more difficult the chores became. In my early teens I was as adept in the kitchen as a grown woman.

And so there came a day when my mother was playing canasta and the housekeeper was ill. It fell to me to complete the dinner preparations. French Fried potatoes were on the menu. I peeled, sliced and fried a mountain of them in hot chicken fat. I dusted them with kosher salt. I was red-faced and sweaty from the hot stove but finished just in time to set the platter down in front of my father's seat at the head of the table.

"Ptui! Ptui!" He spit on them!

My face must have radiated anger and disgust, but I knew better than to raise my voice. My brother snickered to himself. (I could see his shoulders shaking.) As the mountain of succulent golden fries cooled on the table, I quietly asked my father why he had done such a thing.

He told me how he loved fried potatoes and always had. How when he was young and lived in the Lower East Side ghetto, there often wasn't enough to go around. In order to prevent his meager portion from being appropriated by his many siblings — he learned to spit on them.

"Wasn't Grandma Yette mad?" I asked him.
"Sure she was — but I was quick. Had to be or that

---

[*]See glossary.

chazzah* Jay would have gotten them all. Al and Henry, too. The girls weren't so bad."

Sitting at the mahogany dinner table, covered by a damask cloth and abundant with food, it was difficult to imagine my father and my uncles and aunts as little children without enough to eat. I became quiet and pensive.

"Ess mein, tzotskelleh!"* he encouraged me. "I only spit on one side.

---

*See glossary.

THE FIRST CREDIT CARD

It was rare for our family to be all together, but when we were, it was generally at the dinner table. So it was on this night. The four of us — father, mother, brother, sister — and one guest. Grandma Yette.

On the dining room table, tomato juice waited at each place in little iced glasses. When we were seated, the housekeeper served the rest of the meal: pot roast, potato pancakes, apple sauce, salad, a green vegetable. A succession of communal dishes were placed before us that we passed, first to my father and then from one to the other.

My mother returned empty dishes to the kitchen for refilling. Grandma urged us to take more and to eat well. "Ess, mein kinder,"* she said. We ate. We chatted.

My father, often stern, was exceptionally jovial this night. He seemed, in a way, excited. His face was flushed. He teased my brother and me gently and chatted in Yiddish with my grandmother. As was his way, he ate very quickly, wiped his mouth on the damask napkin, belched loudly, patted his rotund belly and pushed his chair back from the table. The rest of us were still eating. And talking.

"You're slow," he said, indicating our half-full plates. "Very slow." Then he grinned and said, " — but while you are finishing, I'll show you something you've never seen before." All our eyes turned towards him. Conversation stopped. With a flourish he pulled a small card from his pocket and held it up towards the light.

"With this card," he said, "I can go out to eat anywhere, to any fancy-shmancy restaurant, even to a night club, and it won't cost me a dime. From now on, all I need is this little card. From now on, no money at all. I eat. I sign my name. I go home. And all my gelt* stays in my pocket."

"No money! Who are you kidding?" replied my brother, a skeptical teenager.

"Enough with the nonsense, Dan," cautioned my mother.

Grandma, on her way into the kitchen for the fruit compote and angel cake, looked over her shoulder and shrugged. She was used to her madcap son. His

---

*See glossary.

exaggerations. His American ways. Her look said it all quite clearly: one more of his jokes. Better she should ignore it.

"Diner's Club," said my father, liking the phrase and repeating it. "It's called the Diner's Club."

We got out of our seats and clustered around his chair at the head of the table. Ignoring the dessert. Letting the tea get cold. We passed the card from hand to hand, each one of us reading all that was printed on it, front and back. My father held forth.

"Anything on the menu, I can eat. The finest. Any drink from the bar, I can have. The very best. On my word and on my signature alone."

In the face of our probing questions, he eventually admitted that once a month a bill would come in the mail that he would pay by check.

"A tax advantage," he said.

As a family, we were awed and impressed. I, the youngest, had of course never heard of such a thing. And further, I was far too unsophisticated to recognize the onset of the phenomenon that was to change the way Americans would view and spend their money in years to come. I thought this was something special for us. For our father, because he was who he was. For our family, because we were who we were.

The phone rang; it was my aunt. I was bubbling with the news and told her everything, detail by detail.

"A miracle," she said.

"Yes, a miracle," I repeated.

"Meshuggeh,"* muttered Grandma Yette.

_____

*See glossary.

19

CHANUKAH*

Chanukah — The Festival of Lights — is the holiday that comes towards the end of the calendar year. Sometimes it's at the same time as Christmas, sometimes not. It's a joyful time, especially for the children, who are given gifts for seven or eight days in a row. At least, that's the way I remember it.

Most of the holidays that we celebrated during my childhood, in the 1930s and 40s, seemed special to me because that was when our extended families gathered to

---

*See glossary.

mark the occasions and to break bread together. Sometimes they talked in several languages at the same time. Drank wine. Laughed a lot. And ate and ate and ate.

One year Chanukah was celebrated at my Aunt Dorothy's house. My father's side of the family. The Romanians. The next year, it was at another aunt's house. My mother's side of the family. The Russians. Of course I did not understand then, as I do now, the delicate politics that must have been involved. Oy Vey!*

Regardless of where the dinner was held, certain protocols were religiously followed. Grown ups sat at the "big" table. Kids sat at the "little" one. Grown ups had the best china and stemmed glasses filled with sweet ruby-red wine. Kids had kitchen dishes, jelly glasses and grape juice. And, as tradition dictated, we always ate latkes* — hot, crispy potato pancakes fried in delicious yellow schmaltz.* They smelled as good as they tasted and were traditionally accompanied by cold, creamy smetana* and, sometimes, apple sauce. Our mouths were watering as the platters came to the table.

My maternal aunt lived in an elegant apartment house in Manhattan with a uniformed doorman who tipped his hat and greeted me whenever I entered. "Good evening, miss." (I never knew what to say in return.) We went upstairs in a creaky elevator to an apartment with the largest living room and the biggest Oriental rug that I had ever seen. And the smallest kitchen. However, my aunt and two maids, in matching gray and white uniforms, turned out scrumptious food in those tight quarters.

---

*See glossary.

The cousins I sat with at the kids' table seemed "snobby" and somewhat bored. They acted as if they didn't want to be there. (Despite the delicious food, I didn't always want to be there, either.) The atmosphere was formal, even stodgy. We were always being reminded, by one adult or another, to sit up straight and not spill things on our good clothes, or on the lace tablecloth.

The most fun came when my uncle drank too much wine. Then he would dance by himself in the middle of the room, holding up the edges of his jacket as if it was a skirt, singing French songs from the first World War like "Mademoiselle from Armentieres." My aunt was definitely not thrilled. She bit her lips and pretended to ignore his antics.

With my father's family, things were not so fancy. The dishes didn't all match. There were more cousins at the kids' table. We whispered to each other, told stories, played jokes and, in general, had fun and got "in trouble." My father and his brothers laughed a lot and tried to play jokes on Grandma but she was too slick to fall for them. That made us all laugh even more. (I remember once when my father snuck into the kitchen when he thought she wasn't looking. He buried his cigar under the pot roast in one of the enormous serving platters. With her face a perfect "dead pan," Grandma ceremoniously served it to him, liberally covered with rich brown gravy. A $5.00 cigar! She really had the last laugh that time!)

Grandma and two of my aunts did the serving. There was a portion of ice-cold gefilte* fish waiting at each place

_____

*See glossary.

when we sat down to the table. This was invariably served on a lettuce leaf with bits of jelly-like aspic clinging to it and garnished with a slice of carrot. Then, steaming bowls of chicken soup with matzoh* balls were served. A dish piled high with extra matzoh balls was passed around and around the tables until it was empty. After that there were platters of roast chickens — the big ones called capons — accompanied by bowls of stuffing and gravy. And pot roast — because there was always pot roast. And things like potato kugle* and a special holiday dish called tsimmes* — a honey-glazed mixture of sweet potatoes, carrots and prunes.

By the time we got to the dessert, we were too full to eat it, but there was dried fruit, an assortment of nuts and candy, honey cake and macaroons. Platters of it. Enough to nibble on for the rest of the night. Grandma drank steaming hot tea from a glass, sipping it through a sugar cube that she held between her teeth. We kids were allowed to try it that way, also. Even though we often spilled it and made a mess, nobody scolded us. In fact, everybody laughed.

The room was hot and full of good smells, low chuckles and the murmurs of satiated, happy people. The younger children began to grow drowsy. My littlest cousins took turns resting their golden curls against my arm, dozing off.

It was then that the grown ups talked about what was happening to the Jews in Europe. The older kids listened. Nobody laughed.

*See glossary.

20

SALLY

My mother's name was Sally.

At home, on any ordinary day, she was nothing special to look at: a Russian immigrant woman only four foot ten inches tall, with a very large bosom that gave her an unusual top heavy appearance. Her brown hair was thin and wispy and usually rolled up in curlers. In general, she was unsure of herself and rather tentative about life. Not inclined to spend money on clothes "to wear around the house," she would make schmattes* out of her old "dressy" clothes decorated with beaded butterflies or satin ruffles. They didn't look too great with bedroom slippers. But when she went out, it was another story. Then she dressed to "the nines."

She never read a book, just the obituary section of the New York Times. She did this at the breakfast table, emphasizing for my brother and I, the number of people our age who had announced their engagements or who had just gotten married. If their last names sounded Jewish, she would look up thoughtfully and say "— that must be the Tannenbaums from Riverside Drive." Stuff like that. She made the *New York Times* seem like a newspaper in a small town peopled entirely by Jews.

To add to that, in the summertime she suffered terribly with "hay fever." Anyway, that's what she called the constant sneezing, running eyes and nasal congestion that afflicted her during the late summer months. (It was long before the days of desensitizing shots and other sophisticated treatments. We didn't even know what the word "allergy" meant.) But, she had figured out that something in the air she breathed was making her uncomfortable and, seeking relief, went through the long, hot days with a wet handkerchief tied across the lower part of her face. My brother and I called her "the bandit," teasing her by asking what stage coach she had robbed lately. Our teasing brought tears to her eyes. Frankly, she was a mess and we were more than a little ashamed of her and of the way she looked.

She loved to shop for our clothes in stores like Saks

_____

*See glossary.

Fifth Avenue and Bergdorf Goodman. She would look at the merchandise and then turn to a personal contact in the garment center to get it for her wholesale. I spent many an afternoon in "ritzy" department stores trying on outfits and surreptitiously copying down the style numbers on scraps of paper. Her own clothes were usually custom made.

My father told me, when younger, she had been an actress in the Yiddish theater. When she was all dressed up, wearing high heeled shoes and tons of jewelry, you could almost believe it.

The only person she was truly close to was her older sister. Aunt Etta married late in life and had no children. She used to try to boss my brother and I around. In truth, we had far too many bosses.

DIAMONDS

Memories of the jewelry in my family — how it was acquired, how it was treasured, the story behind each gorgeous bauble and finally, how each piece was handed down from generation to generation — occupy my thoughts.

Uncle Harry was a jeweler specializing in precious colored stones: rubies, sapphires and emeralds. He had a little office, really just a place to hang his hat, in a high-rise building on that famous street in Manhattan where most Jewish gem merchants did (and still do) business in the open air. Often wearing elaborately embroidered caftans, huge fur hats and pais[*] — sidecurls — they carried millions of dollars worth of stones in their coat pockets, solidified their transactions with handshakes, trading solely on their collective word of honor.

On occasion, we would see Uncle Harry out there in the street leaning against the side of a building in the wintry sunshine. We had been cautioned to keep our distance while he was "doing business" and not approach him until we got a "hi sign" — usually a smile and a wave. He was such a noted gem expert that when he bid at estate auctions, other dealers would jump in and bid on the same things. If he wanted a particular item, they wanted it too. That would drive the price up. Sometimes my mother became his "secret bidder." In time, I filled that role more than once. In exchange, I was allowed to rummage in one of the cardboard boxes in his dingy office where he kept pieces of lesser quality. If there was something that caught my eye he would say, "Take it, partner. It's yours."

He was one of the very few gemologists who could differentiate between genuine and cultured pearls with the naked eye. When I was really little he started putting a baby-sized genuine pearl aside for me on every birthday and special occasion. By the time I was old enough to wear them, I had quite a string.

In the early days, my mother had just a few pieces of jewelry "from the old country." Simple. Modest. Old fashioned. She garnered a few things from Uncle Harry's cardboard box, too. Nothing to rave about. There came a time though, when my father began to buy her beautiful,

_____

[*]See glossary.

expensive baubles. It was in the style of the times, but also a place to hide money made in his illegal businesses. In the European manner, jewelry was considered the wisest of investments: you could wear it and look prosperous, yet it was there to be sold — liquefied into cash — if things should ever "go bad."

Anyway, her first important pieces were a set made up of a matching brooch and earrings — gold bow knots set with rubies and sapphires. Stunning.

Then my father, doing well financially circa 1942, bought my mother a diamond pin — with Uncle Harry as consultant. I remember going with her to the Fifth Avenue studio of the great Harry Winston, who designed it. I watched as he sketched a concept from my mother's halting description of what she envisioned. On a second visit, he showed us an elegant rendering — a picture of what the pin would look like when complete. He tossed a handful of small stones, fiery and alive, across the tissue paper. Then, ceremoniously, he opened a black velvet box containing the larger stones. My mother was to make her selections as Mr. Winston guided her. "Not the canary," he said. "The blue-white." He used an elongated tweezers delicately to display the largest stone, intended for the center of the piece: "A true gem" he said, smiling.

Our excitement as a family was boundless. My mother received the extravagant gift on her anniversary. It looked like a miniature bouquet tied with ribbon. The tiniest stones, set in platinum, comprised the stems of the flowers and the ribbon. Baby marquis diamonds made up the leaves. The largest stones were the blossoms. We gawked as it glowed in its satin-lined velvet box. My father helped her pin it on the bodice of her newest formal gown. Then he took her dancing! When I helped her to remove it, much later that night, it was warm to the touch from contact with her body and smelled of French perfume.

When my father died, that fabulous pin was re-styled into a modest version that my mother considered more appropriate for widowhood. When my son was terminally ill and uncovered by insurance, a few of the bigger stones were sold to pay the bills. Whatever bits remain are now in my daughter's hands to do with as she wishes.

A part of our heritage.

22

EXPOSE YOURSELF!

When my girlfriends came to visit, after school and on the weekends, we would gather in my bedroom, sit on the bed, make silly phone calls and talk about movies, books, clothes and boys. There was a lot of giggling and many a whispered secret. My mother used to like to be with us and, even though we would truly have preferred our privacy, everyone was polite and nice to her. She probably realized how we felt, since she usually devised some kind of elaborate reason to join the group.

She liked to advise us, telling us things she thought were important for young girls to know. Mostly she talked about meeting boys who would, in time, be the men we would marry. "The right kind," she would say. No surprise there. That meant Jewish and financially secure.

One Winter day, when at least a half dozen girls were in my bedroom, she knocked on the door and entered, carrying a package with a department store label.

"Hi Aunt Sally." Two of the girls were using my phone to call neighborhood boys. Not wanting to be caught, they chorused their greetings more loudly than usual.

"Look at the bargain I got in these sweaters," she said. "B. Altmans. On sale." She opened the bag and spread out three brightly colored cashmere cardigans. The girls enthused and admired.

"Try on," said my mother, nodding to me.

I stripped to my bra and slip and put my arms in the sleeves, but reversed, so that the cardigan buttoned down the back rather than the front.

"Such mishagas.* Why do you always do that?"

There was no answer to that question. I shrugged. It just was "our look."

My mother went on: "That would be nice to wear when we go to Grossinger's, especially if you wore it the right way."

I groaned, hating even the thought of another family vacation at that particular Catskill resort.

My mother sat down on the bed, settling in for a long visit.

"You all know," she said "that's the best place to

_____

*See glossary.

meet the right young men. The kind you want to marry. You have to go to places like that where our people gather and expose yourself!"

The girls out of my mother's line of vision were rocking with laughter, handkerchiefs stuffed in their mouths. The ones on the near side of the room were red-faced with efforts not to laugh, lest they hurt her feelings. I was red-faced with embarrassment.

"Expose yourself" she said again, nodding her head sagely, never realizing her double-entendre.

23

SALAMI

My father often had reason to be in one part of Manhattan or another. Whatever it was he was doing, he rarely forgot to bring home a treat for the family.

If he was near Chinatown, it was lichee nuts or, maybe, embroidered Oriental slippers or a kimono. If he was Uptown near the fast disappearing Bronx farmland, it could be any amount of fresh fruit, like Bing cherries or golden apricots. When he was near the Fulton Fish Market, he would bring home salted herring wrapped in newspaper and large chunks of smoked salmon. Then Grandma would come over and make pickled lox and pickled herring. She packed the fish in large mason jars with sour cream, bay leaves, peppercorns and lots of onions. We weren't allowed to touch these delicacies until they were officially declared "ready." Pickled herring and pickled lox were served as appetizers or as part of Sunday breakfast. They were mouth-watering. But when he was in or near the Lower East Side, we invariably got a kosher salami. This was undoubtedly the best treat of all.

Our two kitchen windows, the ones over the sink, were bisected by a wide piece of vertical molding. Today we might call this "farm house style." High up on this molding my father had long ago driven in a nail that protruded for 2 or 3 inches. For a long time it was too high for me to reach.

On the nail, hung a salami — a wurst* sometimes 3 or 4 feet long when it was new. Our custom was to slice it from the bottom when anyone wanted a piece, so the salami would get gradually shorter and shorter. When it got to be less than a foot or so my mother would point at it and say "when you're downtown, Dan — " and soon a new one would appear.

In the place where it hung, a long strip of grease discolored the white enamel paint. No amount of scrubbing would take it off. When the painter came, the grease would soon leach through the new paint so that you could see it again. It pleased my father, who never forgot his early days in the ghetto when the wolf of hunger was always at his back. My mother would grumble about the stain on her pristine white molding. He laughed.

---

*See glossary.

"It tells the world that we always have something to eat in this house."

Salami was for anybody, anytime. For between meals. For a nosh.* For whenever. You could have a slice just for a nibble. Or maybe half-a-sandwich after school on white bread, if you were hungry. And maybe at night before bedtime, a big sandwich on a hard roll. Sometimes I shared this special treat with my father. He would take down the salami and cut it. I would make us sandwiches with the special mustard from the deli that came wrapped in a paper horn.

"You'll give her heartburn" said my mother. "That's much too rich."

I'm almost 70 years old and never had a heartburn in my life. I got to be an adult before I ever realized that other people ate milk and cookies as a snack before bedtime.

How sad!

---

*See glossary.

24

THE MALCHEMOVITCH*

It was an ordinary night. Five men and two children, my brother and I, sat around the dinner table. Three ladies cleared, straightened up and made preparations for the next course. Dessert.

The shortest of the men, Uncle Irving, belched loudly. Very loudly. "Oy Gott,* that sister of mine is some cook." The man at the head of the table, my father, also belched. "Yeah" he said. As my mother passed, carrying an armload of plates, he patted her fanny. "Your brother

---

*See glossary.

enjoyed his meal," he told her.

"I heard" she answered, "all the way out in the kitchen, I heard."

At the foot of the table Uncle Julius, my father's oldest brother, called out loudly "Wonderful, Sally. As usual." He leaned back in his chair, patted the sides of his substantial paunch, then opened the top button of his trousers. Looking towards my father he asked, "This okay, Dan?"

My father nodded his approval, opening the top button of his trousers at the same time. Uncle Al, who was not really an uncle at all, said nothing but did the same.

The last of the men, Uncle Henry, the youngest and slimmest, belched the longest and loudest. Resoundingly. Enormously. His gastric eruption echoed through the dining room. The swinging door to the kitchen opened abruptly. Grandma's head poked through. She peered over her rimless glasses at her youngest son. "Sha sha sha, Hencheleh," she scolded.

"It's all Sally's fault," he said. "She cooks too good."
"You want she should cook bad?" Grandma answered.

My mother returned to the dining room with the silver device she used to remove the crumbs from the table. As she brushed and gathered, the men continued their comments and their compliments. It almost became a competition.

"The pot roast," said my non-uncle. "The best." He kissed his finger tips towards my mother.
"Thanks, Al" she acknowledged. She exchanged glances with me. We both knew that Al's wife, a terrible

hypochondriac (who was at home and allegedly ill) barely cooked at all. He ate at our house as often as he could.

"Do you want to leave my brother and run away with me?" joked Uncle Henry, "and make pot roast every day?" My mother tousled his hair as she passed.

Uncle Irving belched again. And moaned. He had eaten prodigiously, paying particular attention to the latkes. (God knows how many of the golden fried potato pancakes he had devoured! I had lost count.) His wife, an asthmatic, was spending the winter in Florida. He, too, ate with us often.

"Vey iz mir!"* he muttered. And then "Oy gevalt!" He moved uncomfortably in his chair. "Better I should die."

"Too much food, Irv?" asked Uncle Al. "Maybe a little brandy to help the digestion?" Uncle Al owned a liquor store in south Brooklyn.

"Good idea." My father got up and headed for the liquor cabinet. He had forgotten that his trousers were unbuttoned and so was forced to grab them with his elbows to save himself from embarrassment. My brother and I giggled loudly and got a stern frown for our disrespect. We shut up. Immediately.

He brought out a fat bottle of French cognac and five bulbous brandy glasses. He placed one in front of each of the men and poured a generous amount of the amber fluid into each. The men toasted each other soundlessly with up-raised glasses. Then sipped.

---

*See glossary.

My mother came back into the room, carrying a platter of fruit, nuts, cookies and Danish pastry in one hand and a footed cake plate holding a pineapple cheese cake in the other. Uncle Irving looked at it and groaned.

"Maybe a bicarb, Irv?" my mother asked.
"Give the brandy a chance first."
"Skip dessert."
Advice came from all sides.

My Aunt Pauline, my mother's only unmarried sister, carried in dessert plates and matching cups on a tray. Grandma carried the steaming silver coffee urn. The family reassembled at the table. My mother asked the men what they wanted and placed an assortment of goodies on each of their separate plates. When she came to Uncle Irving she looked at him with raised eyebrows and queried, "Nu?"*

"A little of each, Sally" he responded. And, despite his previous discomfort, he ate what she put on his plate, had seconds on the cheesecake and took a final handful of Jordan almonds. We all watched him overindulge, thinking our separate thoughts.

Uncle Irving groaned again. Aunt Pauline, his older sister, a garment worker and beholden to no man, said with annoyance "It's your own fault, Irv. You're such a chazzah."* (That was like calling him a pig!) Uncle Irving would like to have yelled at her for such disrespect but was too uncomfortable to do so. He only moaned again, "Oy gevalt" and loosened his pants some more. "Now I could really die!"

---

*See glossary.

Aunt Pauline snapped, "You keep saying that, little brother, and The Malchemovitch* will come for you."

Grandma could tolerate no more. She stood up, first placing her palms on the table, then hitting the side of her water goblet with a knife demanding immediate attention. "No one calls for The Malchemovitch at my son's table," she said. "No one." She was tall, white-haired, stern, and magnificently forceful in her anger. "Never."

And that was it!
My brother and I giggled. Uncle Irv had a bicarb. The other men, and even the women, each had a fresh brandy.

And the dreaded "angel of death" never came!

---

*See glossary.

25

CHICKEN SOUP

On most days, when we left school at 3 o'clock we dashed off to play, our heads full of the excitement of the play ground game ringaleevio — and boys. But on Friday afternoon it was different. There was a special feeling in the air. And a unique smell. It was the collective aroma of chicken soup emanating from almost every kitchen in the neighborhood.

It was the start of Shabbos.* Things happened in a more ceremonious way. Though my family was becoming

*See glossary.

more and more assimilated, and didn't really keep strictly kosher* anymore, some of the old traditions were still in place.

On Fridays we didn't just change into grubby clothes and run out the back door to meet our cronies. No way! After our milk-and-cookies snack we had to bathe and dress in "good" clothes and stay clean until dinner. That was the order of the day — and you could tell my mother meant business!

The best way to pass the time was to hang around in the kitchen. My mother had gone off to bathe and dress and Grandma was in charge. She let us peek into the oven to see and smell the roasting beef. She cut the ends off the still-warm challah* she had just baked, smeared them with shmaltz,* dusted them with kosher* salt and gave them to my brother and I to taste. If we swore that we had been very good in school all week long, she even let us nibble a few of the grivvinis* she had saved for my father. And, best of all, she let us admire the chicken simmering in its pot. We each were given a clean silver spoon and allowed a tiny taste.

There it sat in a golden mini-sea, little claw-like feet upraised, sticking out of the pot — a bowl of matzoh* balls keeping warm on the side. Our mouths watered and our stomachs grumbled. Would 6 o'clock never come?

---

*See glossary.

THE WAR

World War II brought significant changes to our way of life. The very air around us vibrated with a kind of patriotism I had never known before. Perhaps it was then that my family started to become more American and less Jewish. Less European.

Conversation at the dinner table was often about the headlines in the daily newspapers or what we saw in the newsreel, "The Eyes and Ears of the World." We learned how differently people did things in other parts of our country. We became, little by little, less insular.

Stars appeared in front windows of those houses where a member of the family was in the armed forces. As the war went on, we began to see a gold star here and there signifying that a soldier or sailor had been killed. Since we knew everybody in our community, each loss affected us deeply. Kaddish* — the prayer for the dead — was often heard in Temple. As one young man after another disappeared from our collective horizon we became more thoughtful. When my friends gathered we no longer talked exclusively about boys and clothes but more about war and the meaning of life and death. Our mothers were

---

*See glossary.

the same. They spent less and less time playing cards. They still grouped together in the afternoons in one house or another, as they always had, but now it was to knit mufflers and mittens. Because of food shortages, their customary little lunches became less elaborate and eventually had to be disbanded.

Rationing and shortages became a way of life. New clothes were all but non-existent. Tires were by and large unavailable. Gasoline was rationed. We no longer spent Sunday afternoons going for drives on Long Island. We saved tin foil, shaping the silvery paper from gum wrappers and the like into huge glistening balls for the war effort. Homeowners had to install blackout curtains, especially those of us living near the Atlantic Ocean. Not a glimmer of light was permitted. Some of the men in the neighborhood volunteered to be air raid wardens. Wearing hard hats and carrying flashlights with blackened lenses, they would knock on the door to warn us if any light showed. Every night they watched the sky for enemy planes and the waterfront for submarines.

My brother enlisted in the Navy, becoming a radio operator on a destroyer escort in the South Pacific. I got letters from places like Yap and Guam with spaces where words had been cut out by the censors. To the extent that I could follow his itinerary, I put colored thumb tacks in a big map of the world, so the family could trace his travels.

Talk of food shortages and rationing, brought back memories of the constant hunger of the ghetto years to many adults, my father among them. Sharing his plans with no one, he hired a carpenter and had a closet built under the basement stairs. It had a window in it that my father covered with black paper. The walls were lined, floor to ceiling, with shelves. The door was kept locked. Little by little the shelves were filled with non-perishable foods bought on the black market. Cases of canned tuna, sardines and tomato soup. Saltine crackers. Soap. Toilet paper. Commodities my father thought of as the necessities of life. Despite public service announcements discouraging it, he had become a hoarder. I was torn between feelings of security because the food was there should we ever need it, and embarrassment because it was such an un-American thing to do.

A Coast Guard base came into being in the once elegant Manhattan Beach Resort — the hub of our neighborhood — and a Merchant Marine base took over Oriental Beach, slightly to the east. Our waterfront changed from a playground to a military installation. Suddenly our once placid neighborhood was thronged with sailors. They were everywhere. Walking in our streets. Riding on our busses. Shopping in our stores. Tall sailors. Red headed sailors. Blue eyed sailors. Sailors from far places.

A group of girls — my friends and I among them — would stand outside the anchor fence surrounding the Coast Guard base on Saturday mornings our hair brushed to a shine, wearing plaid skirts, saddle shoes and our tightest sweaters. We watched the weekly dress parade when the men marched in formation, counting cadence out loud in rhymes we had never heard before. When they were dismissed, the sailors threw their hats in the air and ran for the streets. They called to us, shouting "doll baby" and "honey pie" and asked us for dates. We giggled. And flirted. It was exciting and fun. But we were still far too young to even think of going out with them.

Soon, however, the men of the community had an open meeting in the basement of the Temple — an unusual thing to do at the time. They banded together to rent and renovate a huge vacant house in the area and turned it into a USO. Were they protecting their daughters or being patriotic? It was hard to know. Whatever the reason, it soon absorbed almost all of us in a genuine communal effort.

A man I knew as "Uncle Benny" became the chairman; my father headed the entertainment committee. The women, in well-organized shifts, cooked and baked. Famous celebrities entertained. Milton Berle. Myron Cohen. Connie Boswell. Kay Starr. There were parties and heavily chaperoned dances. Occasionally one or two sailors were invited home for a family dinner. I remember them as shy and inarticulate with strange mid-western and southern speech and painfully short crew cut hair. In time "our" USO received commendations from several highly placed military and government officials for a job very well done.

Shortly after the war ended, the USO was quietly disbanded. The beautiful old brick house was sold to a family who turned it into a nursery school. The women went back to canasta games and little luncheons. The boys came back home from their military postings, my brother among them. Most of them took advantage of the "52/20" Club — $20 per week for 52 weeks. The GI Bill sent them on to college.

Wartime austerity gradually disappeared. New clothes and new cars were again available. It was a fun time. My father's food storage closet was dismantled and became my brother's ham radio shack.

The end of the war heralded a new era for my contemporaries. Young men came home from the service ready for fun — circa 1946 — and by this time we were deemed old enough to go out on dates. For me, it marked the beginning of adult life.

27

OBEYING THE LAW

My father was a card. A prankster. A practical joker. He would go to great lengths to play a trick or engineer an elaborate hoax. Later, at the dinner table, he's tell us about his "gag." After a particularly successful one, he'd say, chortling. "I got him! I really got him this time!"

As we got older, my brother and I were often the butt of his jokes. Sometimes it was fun. Other times — it could be damned annoying. Even embarrassing. The trick was to try to out think him: to get to the punch line before he did. As I got older, I beat him at his own game more than once.

This is about one time that I didn't!

It was a sunny Saturday morning. I was having brunch with my father in the dining room but reading at the same time. I had a test coming up that occupied my mind. I wasn't paying too much attention to him. (Actually, that was never a good idea!)

He interrupted my reading by loudly slapping the palm of his hand on the table. It sounded like a firecracker. Startled, I jumped.

"There's no one else around," he said, "so I guess you'll have to be the one to come for a ride with me this afternoon."
I looked up from my book. "No, thanks. I'm studying for a test, and later I have a date."
"Well," he seemed extremely annoyed at me. "No date is more important than family business."
"Okay. Okay. But must it be today?"

"Yes, mein tzotskelleh,* it must. There's something that has to be done, and it has to be done today. I won't be able to pull it off if I'm alone. And if I don't get this done right, for once and for all, I'll be very obviously breaking the law. For someone in my line of work, that's not a good idea."

This was serious. I had, only recently, been taken into my father's confidence. I finally knew that the things he did for a living were all outside the law. Professional gambling. Bookmaking. Money lending. God knows what else. I felt a small shiver of dread. What was he getting

_____

*See glossary.

me into? But I knew that I had to go along with whatever was happening. As he said, family business.

"Okay. But can we try to get home before six o'clock?"

"Get out of those jeans and put on a dress. Something that looks grown up. We'll leave here in fifteen minutes."

I combed my hair, switched clothes and tried to get myself ready for whatever was to happen. We got into the family Cadillac and headed West on the Belt Parkway, towards Manhattan. The road was under construction. The traffic was almost at a stand still. I settled down for a long, slow ride and began going over my school work in my head. Actually, memorizing dates and facts for my history test kept me from dwelling on what might befall us in the immediate future. I was trying to look cool and composed. Frankly, I was nervous and scared — and it showed.

Traffic was slow. There was heavy earth-moving equipment parked along the shoulder of the road. Construction workers with yellow hard hats were everywhere. Yellow and black signs advised us to be cautious. The highway narrowed. Giant electrified arrows — blinking — informed motorists that three lanes would soon narrow to two, then to one.

Suddenly my father leaned towards me as he drove.

"This is it," he said.

Then he grabbed the top of my head with his right hand and squeezed it again and again. I was so scared I almost jumped out of my skin. My voice cracked. "What the hell —?" But before I finished my question, he broke into laughter.

My father continued driving. Unwrapped a fresh cigar. Laughed. Pointed a finger at a particular road sign.

"This is the first time all week I didn't have to break the law," he said.

The sign ahead of us, slightly mis-printed, read: SQUEEZE A HEAD.

"Gotcha!" he said.

28

THE MAID'S DAY OFF

Grandma used to make bedspreads and summer quilts out of scraps she salvaged from our old clothes. She had a round piece of cardboard she used as a pattern. She'd cut circles from the various fabrics, sew them into little rosettes, then piece them together, matching the colors. I could see rosettes that were made from the sleeves of my old blue flowered dress marching across the newest quilt, meeting what had once been the back of my brother's Bar Mitzah* shirt. Amazing! Patterns within patterns, forming a unique whole.

---

*See glossary.

Our life was like that. Patterns within patterns, punctuated by meals. Plain meals. Fancy meals. Company meals. Formal dinners. The Sabbath. The High Holidays. Similar foods repeated in a never-ending kaleidoscope of flavors, aromas and feelings. It was formal and ceremonious. Sometimes there was sense to the patterns. Sometimes — one wondered!

My mother was a great cook. She had taught Mary, our housekeeper, how to make most of her specialities and our favorite dishes. However, when Mary was "off," on Thursdays and every other Sunday, for reasons I couldn't understand, my mother never cooked. Never did. Wouldn't. And didn't. That was a fact of life and one of the constant shapes in the pattern of our days.

So, what did we do? There were several choices. One was appetizing. One was deli. This is how it worked.

If it was appetizing, I would have to walk to Brighton Beach to the appetizing store where my mother's order was waiting to be picked up. I loved to do it. The warring smells in the little shop nestled under the elevated train were wondrous, so rich and delicious it was hard to breathe. I would be allowed to take a cab home because the package was so heavy.

Why not? When opened at home the brown paper bag would disgorge smoked fish of all kinds. There was the traditional belly lox* as well as nova.* Smoked white fish. Smoked sturgeon. And something called sable. There would also be fresh cream cheese and the special kind of oily black olives my father preferred. Pickled herring and

---

*See glossary.

pickled lox with a separate container of extra onions in sour cream to be used as a garnish. On top of the package, double wrapped so it wouldn't get squashed or smell from pickles, was a generous hunk of halvah.* As I got older, I could tell by the size of the package, how many people were coming to dinner.

On the occasions that we had deli, it was even more fun. When I got home from school my mother would say, "Wait here for your father. He needs you to run for him." Did I love that! Soon the big black Cadillac would stop briefly at the front door. The horn would blare and I would run. My father and I would go to the kosher* deli together — but only the one that sold Hebrew National products. In truth, I rarely had to run into the store to pick up packages in a hurry. Most times we'd go inside the store and make our selections together.

We'd pick and choose from mountains of roast beef, corned beef, salami, pastrami and tongue. "Only the leanest," my father would caution. We'd select kosher hot dogs, fat knockwurst "specials," potato salad and cole slaw, then delve into wooden barrels for garlic, dill or half sour pickles. We'd buy sliced rye bread with caraway seeds by the pound. When the order was complete the storekeeper would ask "Mustard?" Hardly waiting for an answer he would spoon loose golden mustard onto a square of waxed paper and roll it into a horn and place it carefully at the very top of the now huge package. He had written the price of each item on the bag with the pencil he kept behind his ear and now totaled it with lightning speed.

Then my father would look at me, wink, and ask "A

*See glossary.

treat, tochter?"* Mmmm-Hmmm! We would put the deli packages in the car and walk around the corner to the tiny store under the "El" where a very old lady made knishes. I would always order potato; my father kasha. The steaming pockets of hot dough were put into our hands, wrapped in paper rapidly being soaked through with grease. "Don't tell your mother," he cautioned me unnecessarily. We sat in the car until we were finished eating, then wiped our fingers free of grease on my father's big monogrammed handkerchief and drove home.

---

*See glossary.

29

MR. CHERRY

My father was full of ideas, always searching for new knowledge and ways to "better himself." I was the one in the family with whom he had chosen to discuss these issues.

Once we wrangled for hours about how to correctly sign a letter he was writing to Ed Sullivan because his new Lincoln rattled. My opinion was that "Friendly, Dan" was not the correct signature, suggesting the alternative "In Friendship." He, of course, persisted and did it his way. (After Mr. Sullivan intervened, a half-dozen Coca-Cola bottles were found wedged inside the door on the driver's side.)

Another time, it was about developing memory power. His concern was to improve his ability to correctly remember people's names. Eventually he located a book on the subject and explained it to me in detail, despite my obvious disinterest. In essence, he was trying to make word associations that connected in some way with the names he wanted to remember. Frankly, he was driving me nuts.

There came a time when we met in Manhattan for dinner at an elegant supper club — The Versailles where the great Edith Piaf often performed. I would have been happy with Chinese food or a hamburger, but he had business to take care of in the club. As walked to the door he told me more about his memory associations, pointing out how well the technique was working for him.

"Just watch me," he said.

We entered the club. A lovely looking hat check person took my coat. The maitre d'hotel ushered us to a ringside table. My father introduced me to this imposing gentleman as he deftly palmed and handed over a folded $20 bill.
"My daughter Shari," he said. Then, to me, "Meet Mr. Cherry."
The personage took my hand and raised it to his lips in the traditional European greeting.
"Mr. Maraschino," he murmured.

30

TRAFE*

Grandma Yette had bunions. Her feet hurt all the time. She wore extra-wide low-heeled black shoes that laced up the front. They were very clumsy and made her feet look as broad as shovels. Whenever she got a new pair, she would take the old ones and cut holes in the sides to relieve the pressure on her bunions. They looked awful. My father teased her, then went out and bought her soft comfortable house slippers.

"Isn't that better?" he asked.

She smiled and thanked him — and the minute he

---

*See glossary.

walked out of the house she went right back to wearing her old bunion-savers. It was funny!

As time went by, the family gradually became assimilated into the ways of the prevailing American culture. It didn't happen all at once. One day I noticed that things seemed to be somehow different. We were still Jewish, but we had become more and more American at the same time. It showed in the clothes we wore, the places we went and the foods we ate. It was interesting.

My mother was extremely busy renovating the heretofore crude, unfinished basement into a very stylish "recreation room." She had a small army of artisans working for her. "It's for parties," she said. The walls were paneled and the floor was covered in a slick pale green linoleum. "For dancing," she said.

There was a bar with a mirrored wall behind it and a built-in cabinet that held my father's collection of miniature liquor bottles. There must have been a hundred of them. A bathroom had been added and, at the very back, there was yet another room that was still being worked on. Even though the door was usually kept closed, I could see it was meant to be a kitchen. But why would any family need a second kitchen?

One day, when Grandma was away visiting one of her other children, a sink, a stove and a refrigerator arrived. Ah hah! Things gradually became clearer. One night, after dinner, my father whispered to me "get the package I left in the car and bring it downstairs." Two pounds of bacon.

And so it went. The downstairs refrigerator became

the depository of the trafe.* Unclean foods. Foods that were not Kosher. Foods that had heretofore had been forbidden. Bacon. Pork. Clams. Lobster. Chinese Food. Meat that came from animals with cloven hooves and fish from the shelled creatures that lived in the sea. In this second refrigerator cheese (and other dairy products like ice cream) mingled together on the same shelves as meat. Downstairs, we used the same dishes for everything. People came to visit and, instead of sitting in the formal living room upstairs, gravitated to the new recreation room. Music played. People danced. Food was served. Smells drifted upwards.

And Grandma Yette stood at the top of the stairs. Her painful feet argued against her ever walking down, and then back up again.

"Vat's dat I smell?" she would holler.
"Nothing" we choroused.
"Do I smell bacon? Do I smell trafe?"
"No ma," said my father, with a wink at us. "Absolutely not."
My mother twinkled her manicured fingers at us to get our attention. "You must never tell. She is old and her heart follows the old ways. She would be very upset if she knew."
So — we ran upstairs, kissed her soft, wrinkled cheek, tousled her silver hair and reassured her that "everything was ok." We ran out to meet our friends. Some of them weren't even Jewish.

---

*See glossary.

31

BREAD AND SEX

It was just another day in early Spring. Everything was as usual until third period gym class. I was sitting on the sidelines, excused because I had my period.

Truthfully, we didn't say it that way back in 1943. School protocol demanded that my mother send a sealed note to the teacher, referring to "female problems" and formally requesting that I be excused from "all strenuous activity." Since my mother, still just a step away from immigrant status and didn't read or write too well, it fell to me to compose and type the note that she later signed. I was, of course, aware of the contents despite the sealed envelope but we kept up the pretense on all levels.

At any rate, we never said the word "menstruation." My girl friends simply called it "the curse."

My almost-best-friend, Edie, joined me.
"You too" she asked?
"Yup."
"Stomach ache?"
"Nope."
"Good. Let's talk."
"Yeah. And let's not get caught this time."

And so, trying hard to hold in our laughter, we gossiped. About this and that. About our gym teacher, who looked like a man. About the other girls in our class. And, finally, about boys.

This was a first. It was a topic that had never come up before. We were entranced with it and with ourselves. When third period was over, we still had a lot to say, and no more time to say it in. We agreed to meet after school and, since I knew I had to run errands for my mother, go to my house. Edie whispered hurriedly, "outside the main entrance."
"Three o'clock. See you there."

We strolled through the neighborhood, books in hand and heads close together. The topic, boys, had us engrossed. As we walked through the familiar streets, we seemed to see more young men than we ever had before. Each one set off a new round of gossip and giggles. We reached my house later than usual. My mother was peeking out the front door, frowning. She gave us a hurried snack and sent us on our way to the bakery, agreeing to call Edie's mom so that she would not worry.

"Please tell her I'll be home for dinner, Aunt Sally."
"Okay. But now, just hurry for the bread. A seeded rye."

The bakery was crowded, as was usual at that time of day. We waited on a line that extended well out into the street, smelling the delicious aromas. Yeast. Chocolate. Fruit pies. Baking bread. Time passed quickly. We were deep in conversation. By this time, our topic had shifted from boys in general, to sex, in particular. We shared the little we knew and made some astounding discoveries.

"He puts it where?"
"Where I said."
"I don't believe you."
"My sister said so."
"How does she know?"
"How do you think?"

Our turn did not come until almost 4:30. My father almost always got home at 5 o'clock, and we ate immediately after that. An ironclad routine.

"Hurry, tsotzkelleh.* I saw your father's car go by a few minutes ago" said Mrs. Feirstein, the bakers wife. She bagged a seeded rye bread, warm from the oven, and placed it in my hands. The aroma was intoxicating.

"No cake tonight?" she asked.
"Nah. I think my mother made pudding."

Edie and I continued to walk and talk. We reversed our route, following the same streets, waving at the same people, seeing the same boys. After a block or two Edie said, "I'm really hungry. Can we just eat the end piece off

———————————————

*See glossary.

the bread?"

"Sure."

So we ate the end piece. And the piece after that. And the one after that. We walked slowly, continuing our conversation as we chewed on warm bread. I think we had progressed, amid giggles, into comparative anatomy. By the time we reached my house it was dusk.

Edie yelled "bye" and turned for home.

"Talk to you later."

"It's your turn to call."

My father's car was in the driveway. The smell of pot roast was strong in the air. I ran up the porch steps into the house, and handed an all but empty white paper bakery bag to my mother. One slice left. And crumbs. My mother stared at me, aghast.

"Oy Gevalt!* Where's the bread? The seeded rye? Your father is waiting."

And indeed he was.

At the head of the table. His *New York Times* folded, subway style, by his place. His napkin tucked into his shirt collar. The jacket of his suit on the back of his chair. A knife in one hand, a fork in the other. His new rimless glasses on his nose. His pudgy face a study in disapproval.

"So" he said. "Where's my rye bread? What's up? Feirstein didn't bake today?"

I almost died. Right there.

"I'm sorry, daddy" I said. "Edie and I were hungry. And we were talking — "

_____

*See glossary.

"About what, may I ask?"

I blushed, and stuttered. My face turned crimson and all the words I ever knew left me at that moment. I was speechless. My parents exchanged glances. My brother buried his face in a book. I think he was laughing — but quietly.

"Must have been some conversation," said my father.

My mother spoke to my father. "Sha.* Leave it alone." Then, turning to me, "Now, run again for the bread."

And run I did. Whatever the speed record was for the 10 blocks from home to bakery, I surpassed it. I doubt that I had ever been out alone in the dark before, but I ran too fast to notice. I ran too fast to be scared.

When I got to the bakery, I rudely cut into the line. Mrs. Feirstein handed me another bread.

"Here" she said. "Your mother called already. But, tell me, what happened to the first bread?"

"It's a long story." I blushed. Took the new bread. Ran.

Later, of course, I was punished. I got sent to my room right after dinner. It didn't matter to me at all. I had so much to think about. Very little of it had to do with bread.

---

*See glossary.

32

THE I.O.U.s

My parents' bedroom was decorated in shades of blue and ivory. The headboard of their huge double bed was padded in a shiny light blue patterned fabric, with chairs in a co-ordinating blue satin. The lace curtains at the windows were ivory. The wood of the furniture had been re-finished in off-white highlighted with silver. "Quite a change," I said to myself. I was home from college for the first vacation of my freshman year. The things that had been altered in the house during my absence looked strange to me. And the master bedroom, as usual, had the most changes. The last time I had seen it, it was gray with touches of gold.

It was customary for our house to be painted every second year. Inside and out. The painter, Mr. Freigang, was a familiar figure. He wore a wig and his black rimmed eye glasses were always spattered with vari-colored pinpoints of paint. A neighborhood character but, it was said, an excellent painter. Very good with colors.

"So, what'll it be this time, Sally," he'd say to my mother, as together they pored over fabric swatches and paint chips, deeply involved in their alternate Spring ritual. Freigang paid a lot of attention to my mother. She was a good customer. Whenever she was seriously out of sorts, she re-decorated the bedroom. It was her thing. It seemed to make her feel better.

During my girlhood, the master bedroom went through one metamorphosis after another. At one time it was decorated in grey, with matching wall-to-wall carpet and exciting touches of crimson. I really liked that a lot. Then, during my early teen years, the same furniture was re-finished in light oak and the carpet replaced with mossy green. Now, light blue and ivory. An interesting combination.

No matter how the colors changed certain things remained constant. The big bed. The oversized bureau. The two night tables. Though the lamps on them changed from time to time to suit the decor, the two antique tables remained on either side of the bed. In each was a single drawer. On my father's side, the drawer was neat and orderly and had a spicy smell. It held, mainly, accouterments related to smoking. A few choice pipes. A tin of aromatic tobacco. Cigars. Matches. A gadget that he used to clean his pipes and another with which he punctured cigars before lighting them. Very interesting stuff. When we were kids, and he was not at home, my brother and I played with the things in his drawer, careful to put them back afterwards exactly as we had found them.

The drawer on my mother's side of the bed was a mess. Several half-used tubes of lipstick. An eye brow pencil. Crumpled wads of Kleenex. A nail buffer. A buttonhook. A cake of mascara with its own tiny brush that she used to moisten with spit. A dog-eared address book. And always, scraps and scraps of paper covered with cryptic notes, often looking like they had been written with the eyebrow pencil. Typically, one such note said "IOU STB 32." Or maybe "IOU FTP 97." The little paper scraplets were not constant. Sometimes there were many. Sometimes just one or two. Some stayed in the drawer for a long time. Others came and went. My brother, Arnie, and I talked about them over the years, puzzling over their meaning. When, as little kids, we asked our mother about them she said, "Sha, sha" and chased us away.

My mother's night table also held the upstairs extension of the household telephone. The phone downstairs was in the main hallway and offered us no privacy. Upstairs, we could speak unheard and say what we wanted to our friends, our cousins, the people we were dating. Sometimes our conversations were intense. Emotional. Nervous-making. As we spoke, we unconsciously touched and fiddled with whatever there was at hand. Whatever was in our mother's drawer. Usually those unexplained scraps of paper.

Over the years, neither my brother nor I could resolve the mystery they presented.

"Is she playing the horses?" he asked.

"Nah" I said, "these are clues of some kind, that's for sure."

"You read too many mysteries," he quipped.

Our collective curiosity grew. We continued to use the upstairs phone, to fiddle with the contents of the drawer and to talk, from time to time, about the little scraps of paper. Though we had our own secrets, it was inconceivable that our mother could have something private. Something that she had kept to herself for as long as we could remember. It bugged the hell out of us. One day, with planned malice, we attacked. Arnie, always the instigator, started it off.

"Ma," he said, "what're these papers for?"

"What papers?" she countered. "What papers are you talking about?"

"The ones in your drawer," we both said, almost in unison.

"The papers that have been there forever," I added. "Look!"

I pulled out one with an oft-repeated legend. It always began "IOU STB." The following numeric varied.

"Put that away," said my mother. "That's something very important. A very important document. And it's private. You shouldn't fool with it."

"Okay, Ma. I won't fool with it, but I want to know what it is."

"Ma, we're grown up now, we're not kids. We both go to college. If there's important documents around, we should know about them."

"Suppose something happened to you, Ma," Arnie asked. "Who would know what to do with your documents?"

I backed him up. "Who would even know these

scraps of paper had any significance at all?"

"Scraps! scraps!" My mother was shouting and on the verge of tears. "These are not scraps. They're" — she hesitated — "contracts."

We stared at her. Together. We presented her with our teenage sibling consolidated front. I don't think either of us even blinked. We waited her out. Our mother was suddenly in a defensive position.

"These are not scraps," she repeated, with all the
dignity that she could manage. "These are my
arrangements. My honor."

"Okay, Ma. We realize that. But we still don't
understand what they are. Or what they mean." My
brother was playing the role of peacemaker, while I tapped
my foot impatiently.

"How could you not know? It's so obvious. You two,
with your fancy-schmancy college ways, how come you
can't figure out what's right in front of you in black and
white?"

I had had it. "Enough, Ma," I said. "What the hell is
STB?"

"STB, Miss College Fancy Pants, is Sam The Butcher.
How come you don't know a such simple thing, all the
money we pay to that hotsy-totsy school?"

"Ah-ha! Now we're getting somewhere. I.O.U.
generally means you owe somebody money. Is that what
this is, Ma? Do you owe money to Sam?"

"Of course," said my mother. "How else do you run
a household, I might ask?"

"And the number after that, Ma. Is that how much
you owe Sam?"

"Of course."

"But Ma, is it dollars or cents? Is it 32 dollars or 32
cents?"

"How come I have a daughter that's such a
schlemiel*?" she asked the blue-and-ivory room at large.
"If I died, would Sam care about 32 cents?"

There really was no sensible answer to that one.

----

*See glossary.

It took us quite a while to get the rest of the information out of her. FTP meant Freigang the Painter. And BSM? Beauty Shoppe Murray, as opposed to MTG, which was Murray the Grocer. And so on.

Our poking and prying had exposed our mother's closely-held secret. She was ashamed because she spent more money then her husband allotted her for household expenses, mostly during her re-decorating binges. So, from time to time, she turned to her trusted tradesmen for credit. She felt that she was caught between two implacable forces. On the one hand, she was afraid that her husband would find out about her over-spending. His anger would be too terrible for her to bear. On the other, should something happen to her, these trusted friends would not get paid. So she had devised a system. Fortunately for her — and for Sam, the two Murrays and Freigang the Painter — her system was never needed.

In time, the scraps of paper disappeared. My mother and my Aunt Etta went to Saks Fifth Avenue and bought sterling silver fountain pens and monogrammed leather-bound books with lined pages. My mother's book was ivory, of course, to go with the decor. Somehow they learned what to do and began to keep their household records in a new and orderly way.

And finally, the following Chanukah,* Arnie and I got our own separate telephone. But — dammit! — we had to pay the bills ourselves.

_____

*See glossary.

33

SUNGLASSES

Like it or not, I was spending a month in Florida with my parents. What a drag! All adults. No other kids. Nothing to do but lounge around our pool side cabana. Listening to the women talk. Watching the men play cards. And at night, out to dinner in a restaurant or club with my parents, their friends, and a smattering of aunts and uncles. All grown ups — and me! It began to shape up as a long and lonely month.

I spent my days writing letters to friends back in Brooklyn, making up exciting events and alluding to adventures with boys that existed only in my imagination. Then, on a morning much like any other, I headed for our cabana to claim the lounge chair I had carefully positioned for optimal sun bathing. My father was already there, moving the furniture around, taking over my favorite spot.

"Hey!" Before I could get more than that one word out of my mouth, he shook his finger at me.
"Say nothing!"
I didn't understand what was happening, but I knew better than to ask.

I watched him rearrange the card table at an angle, so that it would soon get the full force of the tropical sun. He and a friend — a man who was not really an uncle but who I had been instructed to call Uncle Mike — conferred in low voices as they positioned and re-positioned the table and chairs. Carefully placed the two decks of cards, still sealed in their cellophane wrappings, in the center of the table. Arranged the thermos jug of ice water. The four tall glasses. The pencils. The scorepads. Then they each examined and re-examined a pair of sunglasses which my father finally placed, carefully, in the breast pocket of his beach shirt.

"Hey Dad — " He turned on his heel, looked at me with steely eyes.
"Not one word. Not a smile on your face. Not a look. Not a raised eyebrow. Nothing. Do you understand me?"

I nodded.

Well, whatever was happening, I could handle it. I knew that the things my father did for a living were outside the law. And truthfully, I was beginning to enjoy the fringe benefits that accrued to being the daughter of a man who was a racketeer, a bookmaker, a professional gambler. A minor celebrity in his chosen world. I liked being recognized in New York City night clubs and restaurants. And I liked the seemingly unlimited funds that were available for whatever we wanted and needed. And lately — just lately — my father had begun sharing his view of life with me and, on occasion, taking me into his confidence. I basked in my new role. In my growing knowledge. In the developing closeness with my father. Listening to him, I began to understand the peculiar honor that existed in the underworld, especially within the loosely-knit fraternity of professional gamblers. The way they did things. The rules they lived by.

For instance: cheating at cards was for jerks. Winning was simply a matter of doing it better than the next guy. Practicing. Developing the ability to move your hands with lightning speed. Remembering all the cards that showed on the table. Counting, in your head, so that you knew what cards had been played and which ones were yet to come. Never speculating. Understanding the odds. And, keeping up the counterpoint of deliberately distracting card-table patter and chatter.

I had been told that a good gambler never cheats, always pays his debts, honors his markers, and so builds his reputation. A reputation that becomes an inducement to those who wanted the challenge of playing with the best, with some assurance that they would not be cheated. Not "taken for a ride."

I came to understand that the people in our world stuck together. Moved fast. Looked flashy. Dressed well. Danced well. Made sure to be seen. To be known. Then, according to my father, the game came to you. You didn't have to seek it. The action followed you. Where you were

— that was where things happened.

That was the credo. And a part of me was becoming enchanted by the values and the pseudo-glamour of the world that surrounded my parents. Sometimes confused but enchanted, nonetheless.

I watched my father and Uncle Mike from behind my dark glasses. Once their arrangements were complete, they ordered iced orange juice, coffee and rolls and two newspapers. They enjoyed their breakfast and read the papers, loudly discussing items of interest in the sports world. They smiled a lot, effusively greeted people who passed, and were quite obviously presenting their public faces to the world. They looked sleek, prosperous, genial and relaxed.

They were soon joined by two other men. One was tall with pepper and salt hair and a lantern jaw. Lou. He had cold eyes behind wire-rimmed glasses, and six or seven pens neatly lined up in the pocket of his sport shirt. He wore trousers and black shoes. The other man, Irv, was shorter, paunchy and almost bald. His wisps of light brown hair were combed sideways across his head. He wore a brilliant flower-printed beach outfit, with matching jacket and shorts and sandals on his feet. His skin was pale; he probably had not been in Florida for too long.

My father and Uncle Mike greeted the newcomers warmly.
"Glad you could make it."
"Pleasure to see you."
"Have a seat."
"Here, take my chair; it's the most comfortable."
"How about a cold drink? A cigar?"

With the amenities out of the way, cards were dealt and the game began. Gin Rummy. Fast and furious, with a complicated triple-column scoring system.

"Will half a buck a point suit you guys?"

"For starters," Lou answered.

He had agreed to keep score. He examined the sealed deck, opened it, mixed the cards — nodding to himself as if everything met with his approval. The cards were cut and dealt. Wise cracks and comments in Yiddish and English accompanied the game. The stakes went up to a dollar a point. Then higher. The hot Florida sun moved across the sky, the shadow cast by the cabana awning moving with it. Soon the direct rays of the sun began to touch Irv's face. He squinted his eyes. Rubbed them. My father, taking the sunglasses out of his shirt pocket with apparent solicitude, said

"Here. Take my glasses; they'll cut the glare for you."

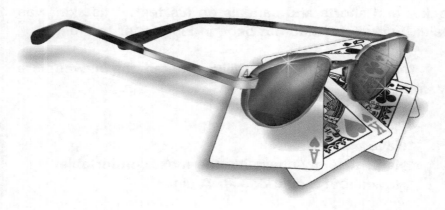

Irv thanked him and put them on. With that simple gesture, the morning's puzzling events began to make sense to me.

By this time I was sitting in a chair by my father's side, watching the game. Just a few hands earlier, he had reached out and pulled me over, casually introducing me to the other players.

"My daughter," he said. "A good little card player for her age."

I sat there in a strapless bathing suit and a starched white pique beach coat. Quiet. Expressionless. I saw Irv, the chubby cardplayer, put on the glasses. The first mirrored sunglasses I had ever seen. Probably the first mirrored sunglasses that anyone at that table had ever seen. My father's hand, with seeming casualness, patted my arm. Held it. Tightly. A warning. "Say nothing!" I now saw what he saw. All of the cards in his opponent's hand were clearly reflected in the mirrored lenses; upside down but definitely readable. It had suddenly became impossible for my father and Uncle Mike to lose.

The game went on through most of the day. At one point, a light lunch was served, with my father playing host. Grabbing the check. Signing it.
"My treat today."
Irv's pale skin began to redden. Uncle Mike offered to change seats with him, to give him the shaded side of the table. Irv refused.
"I've got to get a tan or no one'll believe I've been in Florida. Besides" — shaking his finger — "you know changing seats in the middle of the game is bad luck."

He chuckled, but there was an atmosphere of tension

around the table. Eventually the game ended. Tight smiles. Handshakes. Conversation regarding another game in a few days.

"A return match!"

I watched as an awful lot of cash changed hands.

My father and Uncle Mike strolled to the back of the cabana, out of public view. Together they counted an enormous pile of bills and separated them according to some system of their own. I saw each of them rubber-band a large wad of money. Smile at each other. Shake hands. Part company.

"A good days work!"

"Yeah! See you and May at dinner."

"Great."

As we headed towards our rooms in the hotel, to meet my mother and change for dinner I saw my father, ever so casually, drop the mirrored glasses into an available trash can. Alone with him in the elevator, I began to speak.

"Dad, listen, I saw — ."

He interrupted me.

"So you saw what you saw. And you know what you know. Remember it always. And say nothing! It is not an item for discussion, today or ever."

And it never was.

34

SCOTCH WHISKEY

I was out on a date with the young man I would one day marry. We were in a night club in New York City with two other couples. They were all a bit older — so I was working hard at appearing mature. I wanted to look sophisticated. Worldly. Glamorous. I had dressed accordingly in a black velvet suit with jet beading on the pockets; under it an rather revealing halter made out of black lace. Very high heeled black sandals completed the ensemble.

We had barely gotten settled. Our drinks had been

brought to the table. I prudently ordered the same thing as the other girls — rum and coke. As I was taking my first sip the head waiter came to our table with a small silver tray in his hand. Murmuring "sorry ma'mselle," he confiscated my drink. I was nonplused and embarrassed but tried to brazen it out. As he turned to leave the table I queried: "Can I ask why you did that?"

He looked across the room, indicating with his head that my father and several other men were seated at a ringside table. What was going on? My father grinned and tapped the ashes off his cigar. He mouthed a message to me: "Later."

The evening passed somehow. I was puzzled and distracted. I knew my father could not be objecting to my drinking an alcoholic beverage. That was acceptable and had been for some time. He couldn't be objecting to my date: his parents were friends of the family. I searched my mind but couldn't think of a single taboo I had broken.

A few days later we left for our usual month in Florida. The very first night, my father invited me to join him for a drink in the small bistro off the hotel lobby. We were, as usual, waiting for my mother to dress. When we were ordering beverages he spoke his piece.

"A sophisticated woman drinks Scotch and water," he said. "Nothing else." He paused for a few seconds. "Rum and coke is for children — and the goyim."
"But I don't like Scotch. It tastes awful."
"So learn to like it" he said. He paused again, obviously thinking.
"Sometimes I forget you're such a kid."
"I'm 16, Dad."
"In view of that, I think you should start to drink

White Label. It's mild. With seltzer and a twist of lemon. That'll cut the taste." That was what he ordered for me. His own drink was Chivas Regal on ice.

I couldn't help myself. With the first mouthful, I grimaced.

"None of that. A lady doesn't make faces. Out of the question."

"OK," I said. I was resigned.

"Order it by brand name, sip it slowly. In time you will get to like it. And you'll never get sick. Sweet drinks make you sick. I don't ever want to hear of you being either drunk or sick in a public place." Another pause. "And if that should happen, I will know it."

That was a certainty.

So that was all I ever drank. It made me an expensive date at college when almost everyone else drank beer. But I stuck to it — never got sick, never got drunk, never made a scene. After I was married, and my father deceased, I allowed myself a gin and tonic — then all the rage. I felt so guilty I didn't enjoy it at all.

35

"OH, HOW THEY DANCED . . ."

Originally, our world was a Jewish world. Our friends were Jewish. The merchants we dealt with were Jewish. The resorts that we frequented were places where Jewish people congregated. It was comfortable that way. It was familiar. It was safe.

But, my father, always trying to distance himself from the ghetto of his youth, struggled continuously towards assimilation. He wanted to be a "real American." At times his efforts unnerved the rest of the family.

One summer he selected a vacation site that was new and different. It was not in the familiar Catskills — the Jewish Alps — but further away in northern New York state. My father described the hotel as an elegant place on a lake where we would meet rich and famous people. My mother was distressed at the change, but eventually gave in and agreed to make the trip.

In preparation for the vacation, she shopped. Endlessly. I garnered some new sports outfits, lots of shoes and my first long gowns. My brother and father acquired dinner jackets and patent leather shoes for evening wear.

We made the trip on a Monday, the Cadillac solidly packed with luggage. When we arrived on the shore of Lake George in the beautiful Adirondacks, my father dealt with reservations and accommodations, my mother fidgeted and my brother and I looked around for people our own age.

The first night passed in a blur of newness and exhaustion. It was not until the next morning that I noticed the long porch that spanned the front of the hotel with its phalanx of unmatched wooden rocking chairs, all painted the same color, lined up from end to end. I became aware of the shabby elegance of the common rooms where some things actually were frayed and did not match. And I couldn't stop staring at the other guests — so different from the people I was accustomed to.

In the main these people were taller. Quite thin. With light hair. Red hair. Straight hair. Sharp noses. And strange patterns of speech. They all sounded a bit like the late President Roosevelt and spoke without moving their lips or their hands. This was my first foray into the world of the goyim.* The non-Jews. There was a lot to look at and to think about.

The days were filled with all kinds of athletic activities. Golf. Croquet. Canoeing. Things I had never heard of before. Then, during the late afternoon, the hotel guests congregated on the long porch for drinks. In the evening, a sparse but pleasant meal was followed by music and dancing. The guests wore formal clothes. Long gowns. Dinner jackets.

In the style of the time, there was an American society band alternating with a Latino band. On Saturday night there was a Champagne Hour when the best of the Latin dancers twirled and swirled to the music of the Rhumba. At the end of the set, the orchestra leader would hold his hand above the heads of the outstanding dancers while the audience applauded. The couple collecting the loudest applause was awarded an iced bottle of Champagne.

Up to now, this hadn't been a wonderful vacation. Though the place was undeniably lovely, we remained uncomfortable. The other guests all seemed to know each other, and we knew no one. We sat at our own table in the dining room, smiling politely, having little or no contact with others.

My brother and I conferred.
"Daddy's bright idea," he said.
"We just don't belong here. It's not our kind of place."
I told my father I was "bored to death." He said,

---

*See glossary.

"you'll live!" He had found a few men with whom to play cards. My mother went to the masseuse and the hairdresser and looked quietly miserable. By the time the first Saturday night rolled around, my brother and I were speaking to our parents in monosyllables, making it obvious that we were bored and wanted to go home.

As we took our places at a ringside table for the evening entertainment, the society band was playing. People were dancing. My brother had recently told me what the acronym WASP meant. As we watched the tall, thin people dancing stiffly he quipped, " . . . and that's what WASP music sounds like and what WASP dancing looks like. No rhythm."

The society band finished its set and left the bandstand. The Rhumba band began to take its place, their appearance generating excitement. Dark faces. Elaborate satin outfits with ruffled sleeves. Maracas* and claves* accentuating the four-beat rhythm. A sexy vocalist in a tight dress sang in Spanish, undulating in front of the musicians. The band played a few medium tempo numbers followed by a haunting ballad. Then, a trumpet flourish. The Champagne Hour.

Across the table, I saw my father look towards my mother and raise his left eyebrow. She shrugged, then appeared to acquiesce to his unspoken question. She stood up, carefully placed her beaded evening bag on the table, and moved towards the dance floor. My father followed, smiling, a glowing cigar between two fingers of his left hand. They found a spot at the outer edge of the crowd and stood very still for a few seconds, absorbing the

---

*See glossary.

beat of the music. Then they began to dance.

Like the best Latin dancers, they held their heads still. In fact, either of them could dance with a full glass of water balanced atop his or her head. Their facial expressions were aloof and cool, their upper bodies quiet. But from the hips down, all was motion. Their feet were placed with precision in the rigid patterns of the rhumba. The steps became increasingly intricate as the orchestra segued from one song to another. The beat was insistent — growing faster and faster. At the edge of the floor, I could see my father spinning my mother outward as if to show her off to the audience. He did this again and again. They circled the floor, moving smoothly past the orchestra leader who smiled at them and bowed. Did he know them from other times and places, or was he simply acknowledging their artistry? My brother and I looked at each other and shrugged. And watched.

Gradually the number of dancing couples diminished. Some were tiring; others found it more satisfying to observe. Eventually, only five or six couples remained in motion. Obviously the best. The music did not stop nor did they. It was hot. The lights were low. The beat was frenzied. The exotic vocalist continued to sway, maracas in hand. The orchestra leader beat time on the claves, calling out in Spanish. "Oigame!"* and "Rhumba! Rhumberos!"*   The musicians played through their arrangements, lost in rhythms and harmonics, sweating. The bare hands of the conguero flew back and forth, his drums speaking their primitive language. The austere room thawed, filled with the intensity and sensuality of Latin music. Suddenly — in the dimness there was magic!

---

*See glossary.

And, in the midst of the magic, my parents danced.

My short, plump father in his slate blue dinner jacket with black satin lapels. Diamond studs twinkling in his shirt front. A gold watch. Patent leather shoes. The smoke from his trademark cigar encircling them as they danced. Smiling. In control. His eyes on my mother, as if other people did not exist, but — as we well knew — seeing everything. Executing impeccable, impossible steps. Stamping. Turning smoothly on his heels. His toes. An extension of the rhythm, of the dance, of the magic.

And, my tiny, plump mother. In a beaded blue lace

dress, cut low, revealing the tops of her full breasts. Platform shoes with five inch heels dyed to match. A diamond and sapphire bracelet on one wrist. Diamonds in her ears. No longer the unsure outsider. No longer hesitant and frightened. On the dance floor, in my father's arms and in the grip of the Latin rhythm, she sparkled. Generated excitement. Energy. Sexuality. She was gorgeous.

The music came to a frenzied conclusion. My father spun my mother outward one last time. A finale. He unfolded his silk handkerchief and wiped his face, laughing. There were no other dancers left on the floor. My parents smiled and nodded to the band and applauded their performance. The musicians responded, bowing to my parents and clapping their instruments together. Shouting. Laughing.

The orchestra leader came forward, holding his hand over their heads. The applause was deafening. There was no contest. The iced bottle of Champagne was theirs. They, in turn, ceremoniously presented that bottle to the band. It was the thing to do.

Then, back at our table, my father ordered more champagne. Much more. Suddenly people began to approach us to say hello and offer congratulations. Some remained for drinks and conversation.

The rest of the vacation was a breeze.

THE GIN CLUB

Most of the time there were four couples in my parents' Gin Club. That meant two card tables — one for the four men and another for their wives. The men played gin rummy; the women a brutal version of canasta called "Spite and Malice." On special occasions the games would be bigger. Instead of four couples, there would be eight. My mother had special table tops that fit over the regular card tables and extra chairs stored in the basement to accommodate the larger crowd.

The Gin Club met once a month, ostensibly rotating from one member's household to another. All the members lived in the immediate neighborhood and attended the same Temple. After our basement was refinished into a game room of sorts, it seemed to be in our house more often than any of the others.

There would usually be a home cooked dinner served in the dining room. Soup to nuts. Then, cigars in hand, the men would go downstairs to the card table. First my father would go behind the bar and get drinks for the men — usually scotch. (He generally found a way to show off his collection of miniatures: tiny bottles of liquor displayed in a glass cabinet that was always locked with a key.) Then he'd set up the bar so the men could help themselves to drinks for the rest of the evening. The high ball glasses with the gold bands around them. The matching ice bucket. The seltzer bottles. The bottles of liquor.

The women, who often played upstairs, drank a variety of beverages. I would get their orders and carry a tray upstairs to them, struggling not to spill a drop nor tip over the silver bowl of nuts that accompanied them.

The games would go on until midnight — so, when younger, I rarely was there at the conclusion when a snack would be served. I could here the jokes and the laughter in my bedroom. It was a nice sound, falling asleep. I could recognize the voices and picture the faces of my "aunts" and "uncles" — most of who were not blood relatives at all.

One of the special nights — with eight couples — was in celebration of my father's fiftieth birthday. All the members of the Gin Club got together and bought him a very special gift. A humidor for his cigars — from Tiffany's. It was a mahogany box with a sterling silver lid, monogrammed with his initials, "D.E.N." Inside the lid was a small fitting that you were supposed to moisten daily. It kept the cigars from drying out.

My father died perhaps five years after that. As often happens, some of his belongings were distributed as mementos to his brothers, his son, and to certain special friends. His golf clubs. His miniatures. His cuff links. His humidor.

Years and years passed. Marriage, children, career, divorce came and went. And then, at a family gathering in New England, the past was handed back to me.

In the midst of dinner, a delightful young cousin handed me a gift. It was a planned moment. All conversation stopped. Everyone looked my way as she approached and handed the beautifully wrapped and beribboned box to me. The old humidor. The silver lid burnished. The mahogany patina glowing softly. The monogram still visible. Over the years, I was told, it had held trinkets, decks of cards, letters and, finally, bobby pins and hair rollers.

For me, the memories it held were still intact.

37

THE GOD OF MY CHILDHOOD

The God of My Childhood was a blue tweed suit. With a silk blouse, new high heeled shoes and a matching leather purse.

Every year, as the High Holidays approached, my parents' attention and energy seemed to be focused totally on how we would look and what we would wear when we attended the local Temple. Our family discussions were never theological. We did not speak about the meaning of the Holy Days. Only, would we be as well groomed as our neighbors — especially those who attended the rival

Schul,* one block away.

So the Holy Days arrived. In my teens, I stood outside the imposing entrance of the Temple, showing off my outfit, flirting with the boys and checking out the "conservatives" who passed by on their way to the Schul. If I entered the Temple at all, it was for very short periods of time. To sit next to a friend or the young man of the moment. When inside, I understood little or nothing of what transpired during this holiest of ceremonies. To me it was a mush-mash of meaningless mysticism. Something that was unique to our people, yet something in which I had little or no emotional investment.

In truth, my parents behaved no differently. They were impeccably clad. They showed themselves at Temple, greeting neighbors, doing the proper and expected thing. As an honor — and because he had been quite generous with donations — my father was called to read from the Torah. I remember how he joked because of his ineptitude with the ancient Hebrew. How the Rabbi* had to prompt him. Whispering the correct words. Covering his mistakes.

The day ended with the dramatic sound of the Shofar — the rams horn. On The Day of Atonement one was supposed to walk the distance from home to synagogue. But our car was always parked out of sight, only a block away. I was uneasy, but glad. Those new high heeled shoes really hurt by the end of the day.

That's what it was to be an assimilated Jew, circa 1945, Brooklyn, New York. And now, more than fifty years later, I can tell you that I wish it had been different. A blue tweed suit does not fill the void where God should dwell.

_____

*See glossary.

AFTERWORD

Well, sobeit! Then was then — and now is now.

As I write this I am looking towards my 70th birthday. My colorful father, had he lived, would reach 100 years of age with the millennium; my mother just a few years behind him. The unique yet strangely peaceful world I wrote about is long gone.

Or is it?

I have lived the last 20 years of my life with Jim. A gentle soul. Not Jewish. Our past lives are as dissimilar as can be. Together, though, we have made our own style, our own special blending.

On most nights, after dinner, we play a few hands of gin rummy. Compared to the games I remember from my youth, it goes very slowly. (I call it the geriatric gin game.) As I wait for Jim to discard, my mind drifts to those long ago days when the cards snapped crisply as they were played. When men's fingers moved so fast they seemed to blur. When huge sums of money were bet on the turn of a card and nobody so much as flinched. When the repartee at the table was incessant, barbed, and in an amalgam of broken English and Yiddish.

And suddenly it's as if they are with me — the Gin Club — those card players of long ago. My father. Uncle Izzy. Uncle Benny. Uncle Irving. Uncle Henry. I hear their voices in my head telling me what cards to play. And why. Each one instructing me in his personal rules for survival at the card table. For winning.

"Never wait for the case card."
"Don't speculate. Never."
"Hold it! Not that one!"
"Schtick dreck!"*
"Count the cards."
"Watch the odds."
"Momzer!"*
"Faster. Speed it up."
"Wash the cards."
"Double for spades."
"Gournisht mit gournisht."
"Hold the ace."
"Unload the queen."
"What a schlepp!
"What a mensch!"

They seem so real. Their voices are a buzz inside my head — and when I listen to them I win.

But sometimes they're not with me. Then the cards turn cold. I play badly. I can't concentrate — forgetting whether I won or lost the last hand. And I think: Where are they? Have they gone to the track? Are they in Florida? Or Atlantic City? What did I do wrong? Why have they deserted me?

And then, I don't smell the food being prepared in the kitchen for "the boys." As if, three hours after dinner, they

---

*See glossary.

might starve without a very savory, substantial nosh. The pungent aromas of salami and herring. The sweetness of honey cake. The haimische* aroma of perking coffee. Nor do I hear the click of gold bracelets and long manicured fingernails at the canasta table. Or smell the heady aroma of Joy perfume.

Is this a fantasy or just the memories that live inside my head? Part of my being. Forever.

Shari Nocks Gladstone
Dix Hills, New York
     May 1999

---

*See glossary.

A note from the author —

Working from old photographs, memorabilia, details from the text and her own fertile imagination, the very talented Candace Staulcup has created illustrations that are rich in detail and amazingly true to life. She has captured, in her drawings, the essence of a time and place that existed long before she was born.

The cover drawing of the Brooklyn Bridge is derived from a photograph by the author taken about twenty years ago on a sunny summer day that lives in memory.

And a special word of thanks to Helen Morris, Taproot mentor and dear friend. Her skillful but gentle editorial influence in evident on almost every page.

SNG
7/'99

GLOSSARY OF WORDS AND PHRASES

— according to my recollection.

My apologies to those concerned, should I not remember them as well as I might at this time.

YIDDISH

bar mitzvah	religious ceremony for a boy entering manhood
bema	altar
cantor	religious leader, assists rabbi and sings the liturgy
challah	traditional egg bread
chazzah	an overeater, a pig
ess, mein kinde!	eat, my children
ess, mein tzotskelleh!	eat, little one
forvitz	The Jewish Daily Forward, a newspaper
gefilte fish	a combination of several fish cooked, mashed and shaped into ovals
gelt	gold or money
grivinnis	the crispy bits remaining after chicken fat is rendered
haimische	homelike
halvah	candy made of ground nuts
hencheleh	diminutive for henry
kaddish	prayer for the dead
kasha	buckwheat groats

kinder	children
knishes	pockets of hot dough with filling
kosher	clean, following ancient rules
kosher salt	larger granules than regular salt
kugle	pudding
latkes	potato pancakes
l'chaim	literally "to life" but also used as a toast as in "to your health"
lox	smoked salmon
lukschen kugle	noodle pudding
malchamovitch	angel of death
matzoh	unleavened bread
matzoh balls	dumplings made of matzoh flour
mensch	man
meshuggeh	crazy
mishegas	craziness
momzer	(expletive)
nosh	taste, nibble
nova	short for Nova Scotia salmon, less salty than belly lox
nu?	what?
oy gevalt!	oh boy!
oy Gott!	oh God!
oy vey!	wow!
pais	side curls
rabbi	teacher or religious leader
rebbitsin	rabbi's wife

schtick dreck	(expletive)
shabbos	Sabbath
schlemiel	jerk
schlep	to carry clumsily; a jerk
schmatte	rags, old clothes
schmaltz	chicken fat
schnapps	whiskey, or generically, any kind of booze
sha	be quiet!
shiva	ceremony after burial, like a wake
shofar	ram's horn, part of high holiday service
shtetl	village
shul	temple, house of worship
smetana	sour cream
synagogue	temple, house of worship
torah	religious scroll containing Jewish law
tochter	daughter
trafe	unclean, not kosher
tsimmes	traditional dish made of carrots, prunes and sweet potatoes; also a word to denote confusion
vey is mir!	mercy me!
wurst	sausage
yiddish	the street language of middle Europeans, mainly Jews

SPANISH

claves	rhythm instrument
congos	African drums played with hands
conguero	musician playing congos
maracas	rhythm instrument
rhumba	Spanish ballroom dance
rhumberos	in the vernacular, dance you dancing fools!

Biography

Shari Nocks Gladstone, the author, is a senior citizen and a born-and-bred New Yorker. As a child she dreamed of being a writer but other priorities took over. Immediately after retirement, however, she returned to her original dream. Starting a new career at 60^+ — she has been rather successful as a columnist and free lance writer.

She is the author of *Benjamin's World* — a delightful true-life story of the adventures and misadventures of a cat as he grows from kittenhood to maturity. It is a book suitable for cat lovers of all ages.

Chronicles of Love and Confusion is a memoir. Except for the mandatory name changes — and some vagaries that can be blamed on memories that are more than a half-century old — the book is essentially true.

The author has painted a vivid word-picture of an earlier time and place in history. You will enjoy your visit to that gentler world.

Ms. Gladstone lives with life-partner Jim Tinguely and their two winsome cats. They reside in the hamlet of Dix Hills on Long Island.